# VISUAL STUDIO 2023

The Most Concise and Detailed Guide to Mastering all the Features, and the Use of Visual Studio, Installation, Configuration, Code Snippets Installations, Debugging Techniques, Source Control Integration with Git + Project Management

SAMMIE SMITH

# TABLE OF CONTENTS

TABLE OF CONTENTS ........................................................................... ii

INTRODUCTION ....................................................................................3

CHAPTER ONE .....................................................................................5

GETTING STARTED WITH VISUAL STUDIO ........................................5

*Downloading and Installing Visual Studio Code* ...................................*5*
   Installation on Windows.........................................................................6
   Installation for Mac ...............................................................................9
   Installation on Linux ...........................................................................14

*UNDERSTANDING IDE SETUP* ..........................................................*16*
   Color Scheme Configuration...............................................................16
   How to Customize Your Fonts ............................................................19
   How to Change Fonts in the Code Editor............................................20

*HOW TO CUSTOMIZE THE MENU AND THE TOOL BARS*...........*21*
   The Menu Bar .....................................................................................21
   The Tool Bar .......................................................................................23
   How to Customize Panels ...................................................................25
   How to Add Tools to Panels ...............................................................26
   Visual Studio Document.......................................................................26
   How to Manage Layouts .....................................................................27
   How Reset the Window Layout ...........................................................28

*HOW CROSS-PLATFORM WORKS* ....................................................*28*

*WHAT IS NEW IN THE LATEST VISUAL STUDIO?* ..........................*29*

*ASPECTS OF THE VISUAL STUDIO YOU SHOULD KNOW* .........*32*

CHAPTER TWO.................................................................................35

EXPLORING VISUAL STUDIO USER INTERFACE ..............................35

*UNDERSTANDING VISUAL STUDIO USER LAYOUT* .......................36

*DIFFERENT EDITORS ARE OPEN* ...........................................36

*UNDERSTANDING VISUAL STUDIO EXPLORER* ..............................38

*UNDERSTANDING VISUAL STUDIO MINIMAP* ...............................38

*UNDERSTANDING VISUAL STUDIO INDENT GUIDES* .................39

*UNDERSTANDING VISUAL STUDIO BREADCRUMBS* .................40

*VISUAL STUDIO ADVANCED TREE NAVIGATION* ........................40

*UNDERSTANDING VISUAL STUDIO OUTLINE VIEW* ....................41

*VISUAL STUDIO OPEN EDITORS* ...........................................43

*UNDERSTANDING VIEWS* ....................................................44

*VISUAL STUDIO ACTIVITY BAR* ...........................................45

*VISUAL STUDIO COMMAND PALETTE* .....................................46

*CONFIGURING YOUR VISUAL STUDIO EDITOR* ...........................48

    How to Hide the Menu Bar ................................................48
    Visual Studio Settings .....................................................48

*UNDERSTANDING ZEN MODE* ..............................................49

*UNDERSTANDING CENTERED EDITOR LAYOUT* ..........................50

*UNDERSTANDING VISUAL STUDIO TABS* ..................................50

*UNDERSTANDING TAB ORDERING* ........................................51

*UNDERSTANDING PREVIEW MODE* ........................................51

*UNDERSTANDING VISUAL STUDIO EDITOR GROUPS* .................52

*UNDERSTANDING VISUAL STUDIO GRID EDITOR LAYOUT* .......53

*UNDERSTANDING VISUAL STUDIO WINDOW MANAGEMENT* ..55

*UNDERSTANDING COLOR THEMES* ........................................56

    Selecting the Color Theme .................................................57

Auto Switch Based on OS Color Scheme ........................................ 57

Customizing a Color Theme .......................................................... 58

*UNDERSTANDING VISUAL STUDIO USER AND WORKSPACE*
*SETTINGS* ..................................................................................... *59*

How to Set your Editor ................................................................... 60

Editing Settings ............................................................................. 62

*UNDERSTANDING GROUPS SETTINGS* .................................... *63*

Changing a Setting ........................................................................ 64

*UNDERSTANDING SETTINGS EDITOR FILTERS* ......................... *66*

*UNDERSTANDING MODIFIED SETTINGS* ..................................... *67*

*UNDERSTANDING VISUAL STUDIO TERMINAL WINDOW* .......... *67*

*UNDERSTANDING TERMINAL SHELLS* .......................................... *69*

*UNDERSTANDING TERMINALS MANAGEMENT* ........................... *69*

*UNDERSTANDING GROUPS OR SPLIT PANES* ........................... *70*

*UNDERSTANDING THE EDITOR AREA TERMINALS* ...................... *71*

*UNDERSTANDING VISUAL STUDIO OUTPUT WINDOW* .............. *72*

*UNDERSTANDING VISUAL STUDIO SOURCE CONTROL* ........... *73*

*UNDERSTANDING DEBUG CONSOLE* ........................................... *74*

*UNDERSTANDING DEBUGGING* ...................................................... *74*

*UNDERSTANDING DEBUGGER EXTENSIONS* ............................... *75*

CHAPTER THREE ............................................................................. 77

UNDERSTANDING FILES, FOLDERS, AND PROJECT EXPLORER . 77

*UNDERSTANDING VISUAL STUDIO PROJECT* ............................... *77*

*UNDERSTANDING VISUAL STUDIO FILES* ...................................... *78*

*UNDERSTANDING FOLDERS* ........................................................... *78*

*UNDERSTANDING DECORATIONS IN VISUAL STUDIO* ............... *80*

*UNDERSTANDING WORKSPACES* .................................................... *80*

How Visual Studio Code Workspace Can Be Opened ................ 81

Understanding Workspace Settings ............................................. 81

The Single-folder Workspace Settings ........................................ 81

The Multi-root Workspace Settings ............................................. 82

*UNDERSTANDING SEARCH* ............................................................ *82*

The Advanced Search Options ................................................... 83

Understanding Search and Replace ........................................... 85

Understanding Search Editor ...................................................... 87

*UNDERSTANDING FIND AND REPLACE* ........................................ *89*

*EXPLORING THE SEED SEARCH STRING FROM SELECTION* .... *89*

*UNDERSTANDING FIND IN SELECTION* .......................................... *90*

*UNDERSTANDING SOPHISTICATED FIND AND REPLACE
OPTIONS* ........................................................................................... *90*

**CHAPTER FOUR** ................................................................................ **92**

**INTEGRATING WITH SOURCE CONTROL** ...................................... **92**

*USING GIT* ......................................................................................... *92*

*KNOW THE FOLLOWING ABOUT GIT* ............................................. *92*

*WORKING WITH GITHUB IN VISUAL STUDIO CODE* .................... *93*

*THE GITHUB PULL REQUESTS AND ISSUES EXTENSION
SHOULD BE INSTALLED* ................................................................... *93*

*HOW TO BEGIN WITH GITHUB PULL REQUESTS AND
PROBLEMS* ........................................................................................ *94*

*REPOSITORY SET-UP* ...................................................................... *94*

*USING AN EXISTING REPOSITORY TO AUTHENTIFY* .................. *95*

*UNDERSTANDING EDITOR INTEGRATION*......................................*96*

*UNDERSTANDING PULL REQUESTS* ...............................................*98*

*HOW TO CREATE PULL REQUESTS* ..............................................*99*

*UNDERSTAND HOW TO CREATE ISSUES* .................................*102*

*WORKING ON ISSUES*.................................................................*103*

*UNDERSTANDING GITHUB REPOSITORIES EXTENSION*..........*106*
Opening a Repository..............................................................106

*UNDERSTANDING SWITCHING BRANCHES*...............................*108*

*UNDERSTANDING REMOTE EXPLORER* .....................................*108*

*UNDERSTANDING HOW TO CREATE PULL REQUESTS*............*109*

*UNDERSTANDING VIRTUAL FILE SYSTEM*.................................*110*

*UNDERSTANDING GITHUB COPILOT* .........................................*112*

*HOW TO CLONE A REPOSITORY* ...............................................*112*

*UNDERSTANDING STAGING AND COMMITTING*.......................*113*

*UNDERSTANDING BRANCHES AND TAGS*.................................*114*

*UNDERSTANDING MERGE CONFLICTS* ......................................*115*

*UNDERSTANDING REMOTES* .......................................................*116*

*UNDERSTANDING GIT STATUS BAR ACTIONS*.........................*116*

*UNDERSTANDING GUTTER INDICATORS*....................................*117*

*UNDERSTANDING THE GIT OUTPUT WINDOW*..........................*118*

*INITIALIZING A REPOSITORY*......................................................*118*

*UNDERSTANDING SCM EXTENSION PROVIDERS*....................*119*

*UNDERSTANDING VISUAL STUDIO CODE AS A GIT EDITOR*..*121*

CHAPTER FIVE ................................................................... 122

**UNDERSTANDING DEBUGGING** ....................................... **122**

*UNDERSTANDING DEBUGGER EXTENSIONS*............................*122*

*HOW TO INITIATE DEBUGGING* ...................................*123*

*UNDERSTANDING RUN AND DEBUG VIEW* ...................................*123*

*UNDERSTANDING RUN MENU* ...................................*124*

*HOW TO LAUNCH CONFIGURATIONS* ...................................*125*

*UNDERSTANDING LAUNCH AND ATTACH CONFIGURATIONS* ...................................*129*

*ADDING A FRESH CONFIGURATION*...................................*129*

*UNDERSTANDING DEBUG ACTIONS*...................................*132*

*UNDERSTANDING RUN MODE* ...................................*133*

*UNDERSTANDING BREAKPOINTS*...................................*133*

*UNDERSTANDING LOGPOINTS* ...................................*134*

*UNDERSTANDING DATA INSPECTION*...................................*135*

*UNDERSTANDING LAUNCH.JSON ATTRIBUTES* ...................................*137*

*UNDERSTANDING VARIABLE SUBSTITUTION*...................................*139*

*UNDERSTANDING PLATFORM-SPECIFIC PROPERTIES*............*140*

*UNDERSTANDING GLOBAL LAUNCH CONFIGURATION* ..........*141*

*UNDERSTANDING CONDITIONAL BREAKPOINTS*...................................*142*

*UNDERSTANDING INLINE BREAKPOINTS* ...................................*143*

*UNDERSTANDING FUNCTION BREAKPOINTS*...................................*144*

*UNDERSTANDING DATA BREAKPOINTS* ...................................*144*

*UNDERSTANDING DEBUG CONSOLE REPL* ...................................*144*

*INPUT/OUTPUT IS REDIRECTED TO/FROM THE DEBUG TARGET* ...................................*145*

UNDERSTANDING MULTI-TARGET DEBUGGING ..........................146

UNDERSTANDING COMPOUND LAUNCH CONFIGURATIONS 147

UNDERSTANDING REMOTE DEBUGGING ....................................148

WHEN DEBUGGING A SERVER PROGRAM, HOW TO
AUTOMATICALLY OPEN A URI........................................................149

UNDERSTANDING TRIGGER DEBUGGING VIA MICROSOFT
EDGE OR CHROME .........................................................................150

UNDERSTANDING HOW TO ACTIVATE AN ARBITRAL LAUNCH
CONFIGURATION .............................................................................151

CHAPTER SIX .....................................................................................152

EXTERNAL TOOLS AND TASK AUTOMATION ..............................152

    TypeScript Hello World ................................................................153

UNDERSTANDING TASK AUTO-DETECTION ...............................154

UNDERSTANDING CUSTOM TASKS...............................................157

UNDERSTANDING COMPOUND TASKS.........................................163

UNDERSTANDING USER-LEVEL TASKS........................................164

UNDERSTANDING OUTPUT BEHAVIOR .......................................164

UNDERSTANDING RUN BEHAVIOR...............................................167

CONFIGURATION OF AUTO-DETECTED TASKS..........................168

WORKOUT PROCESSING USING PROBLEM MATCHERS.........170

TASK-BINDING KEYBOARD SHORTCUTS ...................................171

UNDERSTANDING VARIABLE SUBSTITUTION............................171

PROPERTIES SPECIFIC TO AN OPERATING SYSTEM ...............173

ESCAPING CHARACTER IN POWERSHELL ..................................175

CHANGING A TASK'S OUTPUT'S ENCODING...............................176

*TYPESCRIPT TO JAVASCRIPT TRANSPILATION*.........................*177*

*TRANSPILING INTO CSS USING LESS AND SCSS*......................*178*

*DEFINING A PROBLEM MATCHER*......................................*178*

*A MULTILINE PROBLEM MATCHER'S DEFINITION*.......................*181*

*CHANGING A PREVIOUS PROBLEM MATCHER*..........................*183*

*KNOWING THE HISTORY AND WATCHING THE TASK*..............*184*

CHAPTER SEVEN ....................................................... 187

UNDERSTANDING EMMET AND SNIPPEST ................................... 187

*EMMET IN VISUAL STUDIO CODE*.....................................*187*

*HOW TO EXPAND EMMET ABBREVIATIONS AND SNIPPETS*..*187*

*USING TAB FOR EMMET EXPANSIONS* ..............................*188*

Emmet when quickSuggestions are Disabled .............................188

*UNDERSTANDING EMMET SUGGESTION ORDERING*...............*189*

*IMPLORING EMMET ABBREVIATIONS IN OTHER FILE TYPES*.*189*

*UNDERSTANDING EMMET WITH MULTI-CURSORS*....................*190*

*UNDERSTANDING FILTERS*..........................................*191*

*UNDERSTANDING BEM FILTER (BEM)*.................................*191*

*UNDERSTANDING COMMENT FILTER*................................*192*

*UNDERSTANDING THE TRIM FILTER*.................................*193*

*USING CUSTOM EMMET SNIPPETS* ..................................*193*

*UNDERSTANDING HTML EMMET SNIPPETS* ........................*195*

*UNDERSTANDING CSS EMMET SNIPPETS*............................*195*

*UNDERSTANDING TAB STOPS AND CURSORS IN CUSTOM SNIPPETS*..........................................................*196*

*UNDERSTANDING EMMET CONFIGURATION*............................*196*

*HOW TO SET VALUE DESCRIPTION* ...............................*198*

*VISUAL STUDIO CODE SNIPPETS: AN INTRODUCTION* ...........*200*

*UNDERSTANDING THE VISUAL STUDIO BUILT-IN SNIPPETS*..*201*

*INSTALLING SNIPPETS FROM THE MARKETPLACE* ..................*202*

*UNDERSTANDING HOW TO ESTABLISH YOUR SNIPPETS* ......*202*

*UNDERSTANDING FILE TEMPLATE SNIPPETS*............................*204*

*UNDERSTANDING SNIPPET SCOPE* ...............................*204*

*UNDERSTANDING LANGUAGE SNIPPET SCOPE*........................*205*

*UNDERSTANDING PROJECT SNIPPET SCOPE* ..........................*205*

*UNDERSTANDING SNIPPET SYNTAX* ...............................*206*

*VARIABLE TRANSFORMATION* .......................................*209*

*UNDERSTANDING PLACEHOLDER-TRANSFORM*........................*209*

*UNDERSTANDING GRAMMAR*.......................................*210*

*UNDERSTANDING TEXTMATE SNIPPETS*...............................*211*

*KEYBINDINGS AND HOW TO ASSIGN THEM TO SNIPPETS*.....*211*

CONCLUSION...............................................................*213*

INDEX.......................................................................*214*

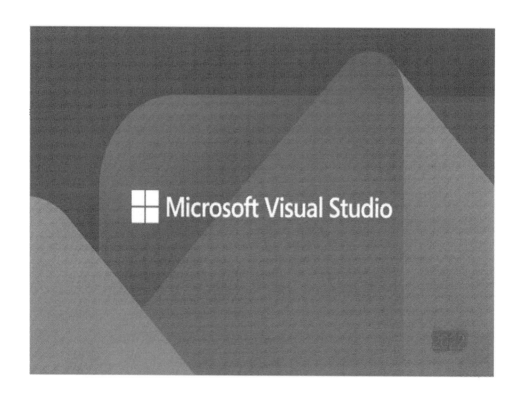

# INTRODUCTION

The Integrated Development Environment (IDE) known as Visual Studio was created by Microsoft to be used in the creation of GUI (Graphical User Interface) and console programs as well as Online and mobile applications. You can write managed code and native code with the aid of this IDE. It employs several Microsoft software development platforms, including Windows Store, Microsoft Silverlight, and Windows API, among others. While you may use this IDE to write code in many different languages, including C#, C++, VB(Visual Basic), Python, and JavaScript, it is not a language-specific one. About 36 programming languages are supported by it. In addition to macOS, it is compatible with Windows.

Microsoft offers an integrated development environment (IDE) called Visual Studio. Websites, web applications, online services, and mobile applications are all created using it. Microsoft software development platforms like Windows API, Windows Forms, Windows Presentation Foundation, Windows Store, and Microsoft Silverlight use Visual Studio. It can generate both native and managed code.

The code editor in Visual Studio supports code refactoring and IntelliSense (the code completion tool). Both a machine-level and source-level debugger are capabilities of the built-in debugger. A code profiler, a designer for building GUI programs, a web designer, a designer for classes, and a designer for generating database schemas are additional built-in tools. It accepts plug-ins that expand functionality almost everywhere, such as adding support for source control tools like Subversion and Git and new toolkits like editors and visual designers for programming languages with specialized functions or toolkits for various phases of the software development lifecycle (like the Azure DevOps client, and Team Explorer).

Since Visual Studio 2015, all versions of Visual Studio have used the same Redistributable files. For instance, any programs made using the Visual Studio 2017, 2019, 2022, and 2023 toolkits can be utilized with the most recent version of the Microsoft Visual C++ Redistributable. Nevertheless, the Microsoft Visual C++ Redistributable version installed on the machine must match or be higher than the version of the Visual C++ toolset used to develop your software.

The most basic version of Visual Studio is the Community edition, which is also the free version. The tagline for Visual Studio Community is "Free, fully-featured IDE for students, open-source and independent developers." The most recent version that is currently usable is Visual Studio (version 1.75) as of the time of this research, which was released in January 2023.

# CHAPTER ONE

# GETTING STARTED WITH VISUAL STUDIO

The Visual Studio Integrated Development Environment will be where you work to create any kind of app or learn a language (IDE). Together with code editing, the Visual Studio IDE also combines graphical designers, compilers, code completion tools, source control, extensions, and a variety of other tasks in one place. We'll start by downloading and installing everything.

## Downloading and Installing Visual Studio Code

No matter what version of Windows your machine runs, use the instructions below to download Visual Studio. Please take note that downloading for a different operating system than the one your PC uses may cause incompatibilities.

- Access the downloads page at https://visualstudio.microsoft.com/downloads/.
- Find the Windows-compatible version by scrolling down.

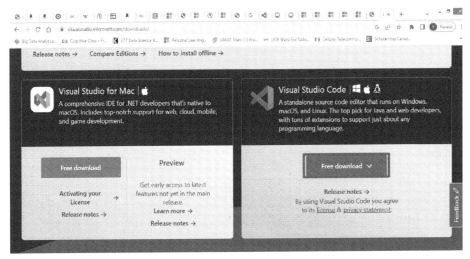

- Click on free download and choose windows the download process will start immediately.

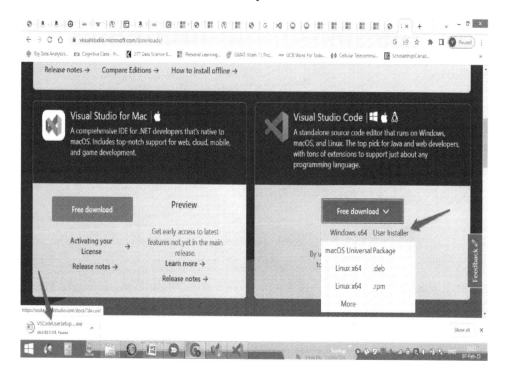

- The download will be finished in a few seconds or minutes.

## Installation on Windows

The Visual Studio Installer can be installed by running the bootstrapper file. Everything required to both install and customize Visual Studio is included in this new, lightweight installer.

- To begin the installation, double-click VisualStudioSetup.exe in the Downloads folder.

- You will be asked to acknowledge the Microsoft License Terms, choose I accept the agreement, and click Next.

- In the following installation window, pick extra tasks, then click Next.

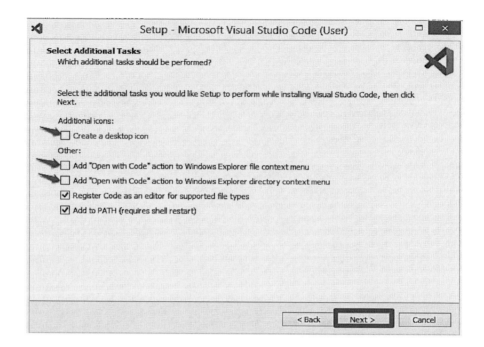

- Click Install in the popup that says "Ready to Install," and the installation will start right away.

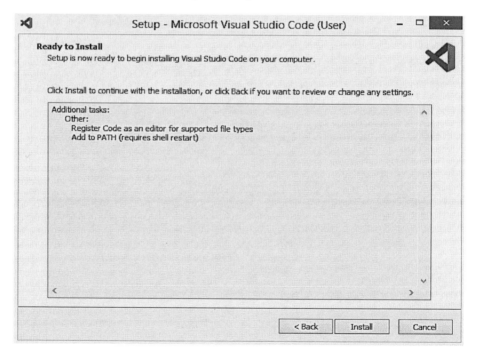

- Hold off until the procedure is finished. After checking, Start Visual Studio code, click Finish to launch Visual Studio, and begin developing.

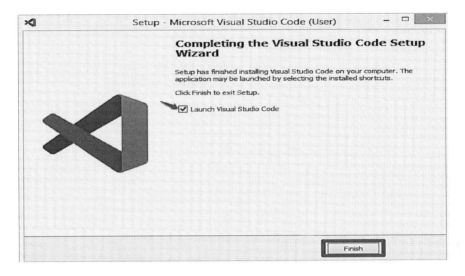

## Installation for Mac

- Adhere to the installation instructions included in the download package for Visual Studio for Mac.
- Click the Visual Studio For Mac Installer build number when the download is finished, and then double-click the arrow icon to launch it.

- The installation procedure can be started by clicking the large arrow.

- You may get a warning that the application was downloaded from the Internet. Choose Open.

- You will receive a notification asking you to accept the licensing and privacy terms. Click the links to read them, then choose Continue if you agree.

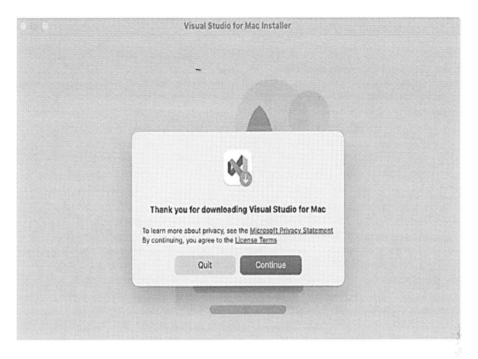

- Choose the "Continue" button after clicking the privacy and conditions links if you agree.
- A list of the available workloads is shown. Choose the components you want to use.

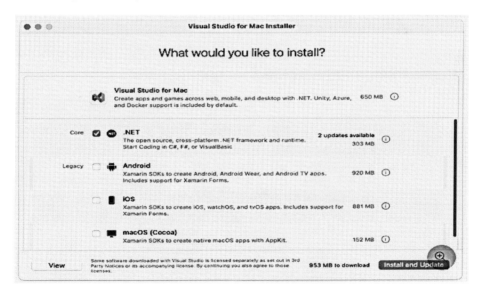

• After making your choices, click the Install button.

The installer will display progress as Visual Studio for Mac and the selected workloads are downloaded and installed. You will be prompted to enter your password to grant the permissions necessary for installation.

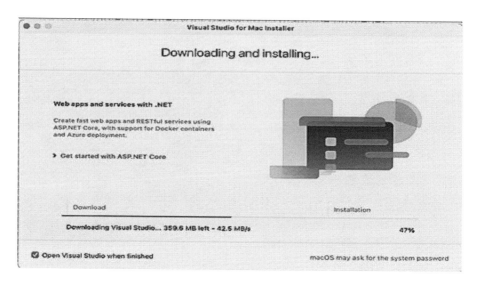

- When Visual Studio for Mac has been installed, it will prompt you to personalize it by logging in and selecting the key bindings you want to use.

- Choose the keyboard shortcuts you wish to use.

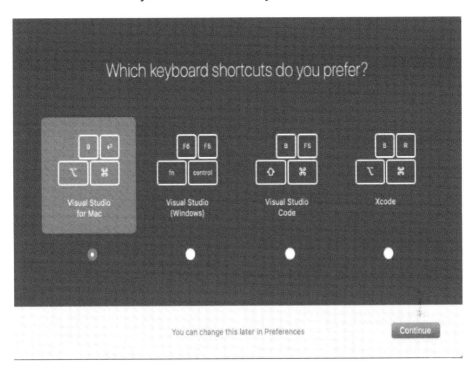

- Visual Studio for Mac will launch, giving you the option to start a fresh project or continue an ongoing one.

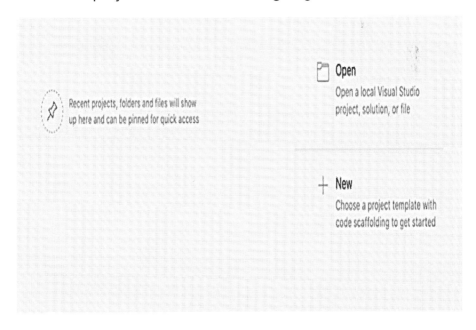

# Installation on Linux

You may install Visual Studio Code in Linux in several different methods. The first approach is described below.

- A Snap bundle is available for Visual Studio Code. Users of Ubuntu can discover it within the Software Center and quickly install it.

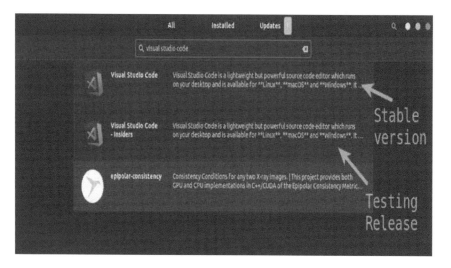

- Any Linux distribution that supports Snap packages can be used to install it thanks to Snap packaging. If you haven't already, make sure to activate Snap support in your Linux distribution.
- Use the following command to install Visual Studio Code if it isn't already there in your software center or app center.

*sudo snap install code --classic*

- A special type of packaging that is frequently huge is called a snap. The Snap package will therefore take some time to download and install, depending on your internet speed.

The second method involves using .deb/.rpm packages. Microsoft provides Visual Studio Code installation packages for Linux. To get the

.deb and .rpm file substitutes for the Linux platform, just go to the Visual Studio Code download page.

- Decide whether to use Ubuntu or any other Linux distribution based on Ubuntu, such as Linux Mint, elementary OS, etc. For Linux distributions based on Fedora and SUSE, RPM files are used.

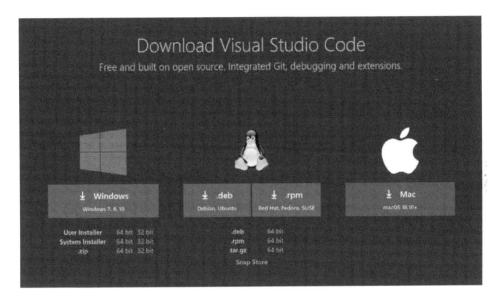

- Moreover, there are choices for 32-bit platforms. If you're unsure, you should check out to determine if your version of Ubuntu is 32-bit or 64-bit, and then download the files in accordance.
- Simply double-click the downloaded deb file to begin the installation process.

The third method is using Flatpak.

- The .deb/.rpm package is the ideal option if you detest utilizing snap packages. But, if you prefer to use Flatpak, you can do so as well. In my instance, Pop OS 20.04 comes pre-configured with Flatpak support. But if you're not familiar with Flatpak, I'd advise you to look at our instructions for using Flatpak on Linux.

- If your software shop supports Flatpak, all you need to do is search for Visual Studio Code and install it.
- Nevertheless, if you don't already have it, you must install Flatpak support before entering the command.

*flatpak install flathub com.visualstudio.code*

# UNDERSTANDING IDE SETUP

## Color Scheme Configuration

Color customization is one of the most important ways to customize Visual Studio 2023.

You'll surely want to change the colors to your liking whether you're in a well-lit region or switching from another programming environment.

There are two methods we can customize Visual Studio 2023's color palette. The default themes for Visual Studio and Visual Studio Color Theme Designer.

1. Visual studio default themes

The following dialog will appear as soon as you launch Visual Studio 2023 for the first time, asking you about the development options and color scheme you desire.

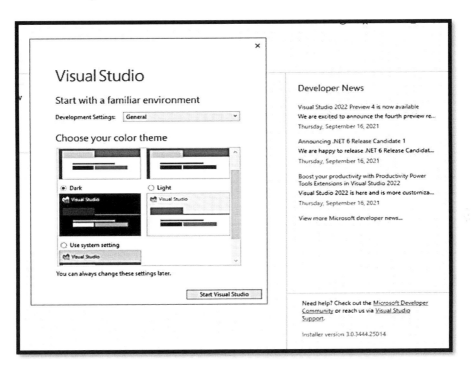

Dark, Blue, Bright, and Blue color schemes with increased contrast are used. The same window can then be used to preview the pre-set colors for each of these choices.

As soon as you make your decision, the theme of your choice will be applied and saved in the configuration linked to the Microsoft account you used to get the license for the use of the IDE.

If you wish to modify the theme you chose at the beginning, open Visual Studio and choose to proceed without writing any code.

From here, input themes in the tools drop-down. The themes that are installed as well as the default ones will be seen there. Then you can choose one.

Goto **Tools**, **Options**, **Environment**, **General**, and selecting the color theme are more ways to change the theme.

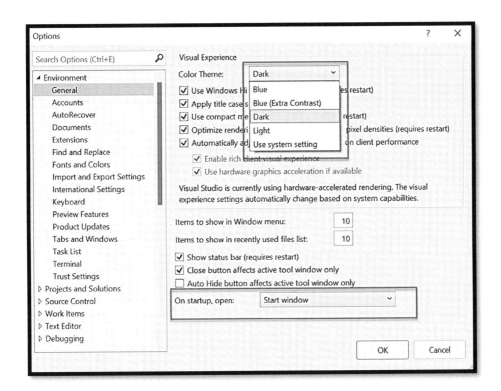

Also from this menu, you can change the way you want the visual studio to start by choosing another option from the section **on startup>open.**

## How to Customize Your Fonts

You might want to change the font type in two places: the general environment and the source code editor.

- Go to tools, then select options.
- After entering the environment, fonts, and colors in the setup window, click OK.
- In this menu, select environments from the "display settings for" drop-down menu.

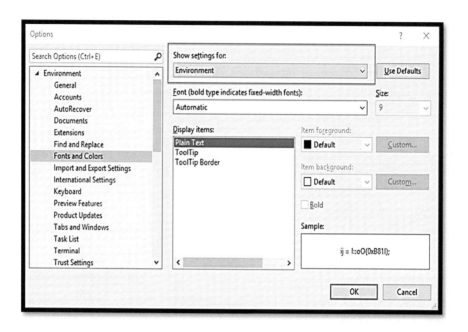

While the backdrop color can be altered in the "item background," the text color can be altered in the "item foreground." The sample option will then allow you to see the color you selected in advance.

## How to Change Fonts in the Code Editor

You must next follow the steps outlined above to modify the fonts inside the code editor. As part of the setup options, you can change the background color, text size, font color, and other characteristics.

One advantage of employing this configuration option is the capacity to tailor the setup to your precise requirements. The implication is that, in addition to a wide range of other settings, you may modify the typography for things like line numbers, bookmarks, selected text, and code snippets.

Now that you know how to alter the font to suit your needs, let's look at how to modify the panels within the IDE so that your workflow will be quicker after your projects.

# HOW TO CUSTOMIZE THE MENU AND THE TOOLBARS

The greatest places to find tools or frequently used commands are the menu bars and toolbars. Then, to create the application, it is crucial to learn how to customize these items. We will thus go over how to alter the menu bar and the toolbar in this part.

## The Menu Bar

The menu bar is a collection of options that displays at the top of the IDE and allows you to access a drop-down menu of options (like the File menu) to perform a specific task, display tools, or modify a project:

If you want to change the tools that are included in the default configuration, either to add options to a specific menu or to make your menus, you must do the steps stated below:

- Open the tools menu and select customize.
- See the Commands section.
- To modify the primary menu bar and the secondary menu bar, which are identified by pipe symbols (|) in the dropdown, utilize the Menu bar option in this section.

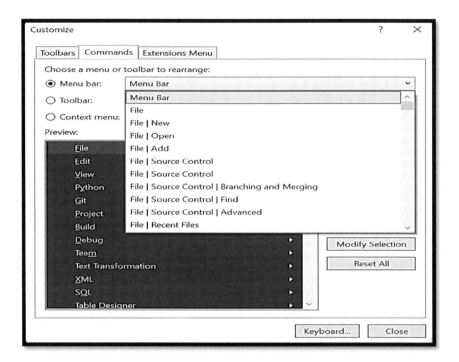

- You will receive a preview of the menu once you have decided which one you wish to customize. When you choose add command, a new command will appear in the menu bar. this brings up a new window where you may select and add commands to the menu of your choice. The commands are grouped by category.

- Choose the newly added item, then delete it to remove it from the menu. The menu's buttons also allow you to scroll up and down.

- Lastly, you may also design menus and submenus. Choose add a new menu to get started. Depending on the hierarchy level you are in, this adds a new menu.

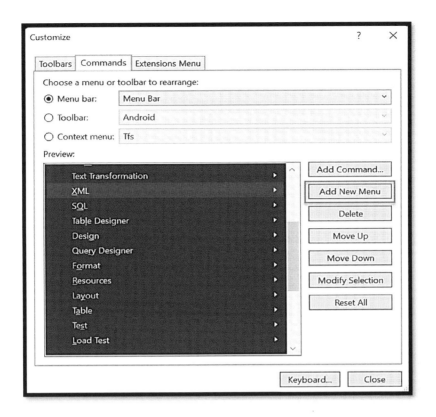

Alternately, when selecting the edit menu, you must complete the preceding step to add a submenu.

## The Tool Bar

You can access the group of commands on the toolbar without first opening the menu. You can also pick which commands will be displayed in which tool groups by clicking Tools, then Customize. The numerous categories we may select to show in the user interface will by default be displayed on the Toolbars tab in this window. Standard is automatically selected for API and web apps. Depending on the project, other toolbars might be provided by default, but we can manually add additional toolbars by simply selecting them with a tick.

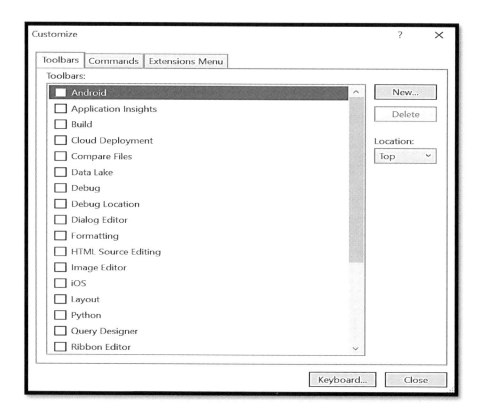

You can add more commands to a toolbar by choosing the Commands tab. Following the same steps as in the section on customizing the menu bar, we will select the toolbar we want to change in this tab.

The image below shows you how to access the View menu and Toolbars, where you may select and deselect the toolbars you want to add to the IDE right away.

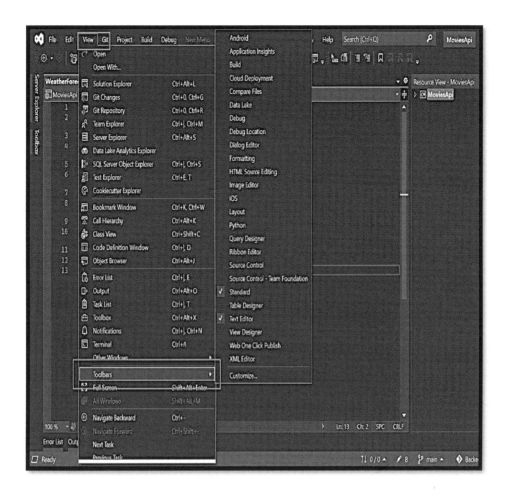

## How to Customize Panels

Depending on the type of project you are working on, you may be able to access various tools in Visual Studio panels.

These panels are made up of document editors and tools, some of which are frequently used, including the solution explorer (to view the structure of your projects), the toolbox (which displays controls to drag and drop according to the current project), the properties panel (to change the properties of the selected element), and the code editor.

We'll walk you through several key customizing panel topics in this section.

# How to Add Tools to Panels

You can discover a few tools or windows on the view menu that you can display or conceal.

When you open this menu, the most frequently used tools are displayed right away. These tools include the server explorer, the class viewer, the output window, the terminal, and the error listing, among other powerful ones. Another group of instruments, however less common, may at some point become valuable to you. You can find these under "Other Windows."

The Package Manager Console, Data Sources, C# interactive, and containers, among other tools, are accessible via this page. Simply pick one of these tools and add it to a panel; it will then be strategically incorporated into your current surroundings. For example, if you add the Server Explorer tool, it will be added to the left panel. On the other hand, if you add the Output tool, it will be added to the bottom pane.

One of the numerous advantages of Visual Studio is the freedom to arrange the tool panels in any way you choose. Understanding how a panel is put together will help you achieve the optimum results.

Each panel has five spaces where you can place tools. These sections are located on either side of the panel, with one in the middle.

To put the tool into a panel, simply move the cursor to the chosen panel by locating it at the tool's top. The IDE will automatically recommend possible locations for the tool, simplifying and speeding up the process. Even better, you can use the panel on its own without the main windows.

# Visual Studio Document

If you are using a document editor like the code editor, you have a few choices that you can add. Simply right-click on the document's tab to access this option.

These options are quite easy to use; for example, choosing Float will turn the editor into a floating window that we may move to another monitor. The Set Tab Layout option allows us to move the tab group to the left, top, or right while the Pin Tab option places the tab at the top of all open windows.

It is essential to stress that if we have more documents open, we will have access to more options. By selecting this option, we may divide up the space for documents into groups so that we can utilize it for tasks that will increase productivity, such as comparing two documents.

## How to Manage Layouts

You could work on a range of projects as a developer. In general, you should always have the Server Explorer tool open in case you need to manage database-related duties for a project.

Keep your toolbox open in case you need to use databases for another project you're working on at the same time. Many tasks are connected to the arrangement of the windows. Here they are.

**You can save the layout.**

After setting up your panels with the tools required for a certain project, you must choose Window, then Save Window Layout.

You will be prompted to name your workspace setup in a new window that will open. The setting is immediately saved as soon as you enter a name.

Choose "Manage Window Layouts" from the Window menu. Upon doing so, a popup containing all of your previously saved workspaces or layouts will appear, allowing you to verify the modification.

You can use it to load the panels with the tools in your workspace in the same order as when you last saved the window layout once you've saved at least one layout.

You need to apply a layout after choosing the Apply Window Layout option in the Window menu, which shows all previously saved layouts. When you select the workspace you want to utilize, it will load.

## How to Reset the Window Layout

Lastly, you might want to undo any changes you've made to a workspace so that Visual Studio returns to its factory settings. Thankfully, choosing Window > Reset Window Layout from the menu will give you access to this choice.

A prompt will show up when we click this button asking if we want to return to the default settings. The environment will be enabled with its default settings if "Yes" is simply selected.

# HOW CROSS-PLATFORM WORKS

A cross-platform application can run on Linux, macOS, and Windows. Software may support more than two platforms, or it may only support two. A few cross-platform development frameworks are Codename One, Kivy, Qt, Flutter, NativeScript, Xamarin, PhoneGap, Ionic, and React Native.

You can deploy your cross-platform apps to different Android device setups using Visual Studio. Your cross-platform C++, Xamarin, or Cordova projects can use it. The Visual Studio Emulator for Android can be installed under Individual components using the most recent version of Visual Studio.

# WHAT IS NEW IN THE LATEST VISUAL STUDIO?

Welcome to the Windows, Mac, and Linux versions of Visual Studio Code as of January 2023. We hope you enjoy the numerous updates in this edition, some of which are as follows:

- Profiles: To customize extensions, settings, shortcuts, and other features, and create and share profiles.
- Code signing is now the default for published extensions on the Visual Studio Marketplace.
- Accessibility enhancements: screen reader mode for the terminal, and new keyboard shortcuts.
- Drag layout corners to resize many views at once for easier multi-view resizing.
- Tree view search history: Immediately do past tree view searches.
- Improved Terminal link detection: Look for connections with spaces, brackets, line breaks, and column formats.
- The new Git commands to store staged changes and delete remote tags are now supported by Visual Studio Code.
- Please try out the experimental Dark+ and Light+ V2 color schemes and let us know what you think.
- Jupyter Notebook topics include managing Jupyter kernels and using notebooks online.
- Visual Studio Code's AI Tools: Read more about GitHub Copilot's AI-powered completions.
- Performance Enhancements: Visual Studio 2023 is quicker, more user-friendly, and lighter, and it is created for both beginners and developers of large-scale industrial applications.

- Visual Studio 2023 is 64-bit: A 64-bit version of Visual Studio 2023 for Windows is now available. This means that even the largest and most complex solutions can be opened, edited, run, and debugged without running out of memory.
- Faster Find in Files: With Visual Studio 2023, we concentrated on enhancing the performance of several essential functionalities. For instance, when looking for huge solutions like Orchard Core, Search in Files is currently up to 3 times faster. Locating Files is now even quicker thanks to improved indexed searching.
- New Git Feature: The commit graph is a new Git feature that enhances both the efficiency of your Git operations and that of Visual Studio.
- Develop cutting-edge apps: Visual Studio 2023 and Azure let you easily develop modern, cloud-based applications. Also, our updated version now offers full .NET and its unified framework for web, client, and mobile app compatibility for both Mac and Windows developers. Moreover, C++ workload support has been improved in Visual Studio 2023 with the addition of new productivity tools, C++ 20 tooling, and IntelliSense.
- Visual Studio 2023 now has enhanced cross-platform app development features and the most recent C++ build tools now support C++ 20.
- Better dev tools for C++ and .NET, as well as Hot Reload. You can edit C++ or .NET projects while your program is running by using Hot Reload.
- Improvements to the Blazor and Razor editors as well as Hot Reload for ASP.NET: Visual Studio 2023 offers significant updates to the Blazor and Razor editors as well as new features for Hot Reload in ASP.NET Core, such as Hot Reload when a file is saved or when CSS changes are made in real-time.
- Innovation at your fingertips: Visual Studio 2023 offers all of this and more, including real-time and asynchronous collaborative

- tools, better insights, and productivity tools that easily integrate with your daily workflow.
- Support for multiple Git repositories and line staging: If you've worked on projects that were hosted in different Git repositories, you might have connected to them using other software or numerous instances of Visual Studio. You can now work with a single solution that incorporates projects in several repositories and contribute to them all from a single instance of Visual Studio.
- Line staging, often known as interactive staging support, has been added. Now you may break your changes into numerous commits or stage portions of them right from the code editor.
- Whole line completion: The IntelliCode tool in Visual Studio 2023 may now automatically complete up to a whole line of code at once.
- IntelliCode can now recognize when you're conducting a routine activity and suggest the appropriate Quick Action, completing it as you type.
- Designed for everyone: The implementation of a new user interface will help you stay more in the zone. Cosmetic adjustments that modernize the user interface or ease congestion are some of the changes.
- Appearance and feel: New Cascadia Code typeface, revised iconography, and minor color contrast ratio adjustments have made Visual Studio 2023 more user-friendly.
- Customization and personalization: We worked hard to make Visual Studio more adaptable and personalized so you could make the IDE your own. For instance, Visual Studio 2023 allows you to sync with your Windows theme. Because of this, if you've turned on the "night light" feature in Visual Studio, it is also utilized there.

# ASPECTS OF THE VISUAL STUDIO YOU SHOULD KNOW

Below are the basic features available to developers using Visual Studio.

- **Modular installation**: With the modular installer in Visual Studio, you choose and install the workloads you need. Workloads are groups of features needed for a platform's or a programming language's functionality. A modular strategy can make installing and updating Visual Studio quicker and less harmful to the environment.
- **Build cloud-enabled Azure apps:** Building cloud-enabled applications for Microsoft Azure is made simple with the help of several tools included with Visual Studio. It is possible to configure, build, debug, package, and deploy Azure apps and services directly from the Visual Studio integrated development environment (IDE). Choose the Azure development workload when installing Visual Studio to get the Azure tools and project templates. When necessary, you can either use the Azure portal or the Azure node of Server Explorer included in older releases of Visual Studio. You can leverage Azure services for your apps and Azure Active Directory (Azure AD) accounts to connect to online apps by including Connected Services, such as Active Directory Connected Service. Use Azure Storage for blob storage, queues, tables, and related services for Key Vault to manage secrets for web apps. The Connected Services available depend on the project category. To add a service, right-click the project in Solution Explorer and choose Add > Connected Service. To add a service dependency on the Connected Services screen, select the link or the plus sign. On the Add Dependence box, select the service you want to add.

Then, follow the on-screen directions to connect to your Azure membership and service.

- **Write web applications**: You may use Visual Studio to help you create web applications. To create web applications, use ASP.NET, Node.js, Python, JavaScript, and TypeScript. Visual Studio supports a wide range of web frameworks, including Angular, jQuery, and Express. Both ASP.NET Core and .NET Core are supported by Windows, MacOS, and Linux operating systems. ASP.NET Core represents a significant upgrade to MVC, WebAPI, and SignalR. The lean and modular.NET framework made available by ASP.NET Core can be used to create contemporary cloud-based web apps and services.

- **Create cross-platform apps and games**: You can make apps and games with Visual Studio for mobile devices as well as for Windows, Linux, macOS, Android, and other operating systems. Using Visual Studio, .NET Core apps may be created for Windows, macOS, and Linux. Apps produced in C# and F# using Xamarin, native C++ applications for iOS, Android, and Windows platforms, and 2D and 3D games written in C# using Visual Studio Tools for Unity Libraries for iOS, Android, and Windows can exchange code thanks to the use of C++ for cross-platform development.

- **Connect to databases**: Using Server Explorer, you can browse and manage server instances and resources on websites, Azure, Microsoft 365, Salesforce.com, and other platforms as well as locally and remotely. To open Server Explorer, select View > Server Explorer. Go here to learn more about using Server Explorer. Similar to SQL Server Management Studio, SQL Server Object Explorer offers a view of your database objects. SQL Server Object Explorer lets you do basic database administration and design activities. Contextual menus can be used, among other things, to perform queries, edit table data, and compare schemas. To open SQL Server Object Explorer, either click the icon for it at the top of the Server Explorer window or select View > SQL Server Object Explorer from the Visual Studio top menu. SQL Server Data Tools provides a powerful development environment for SQL Server, Azure SQL Database, and Azure SQL Data Warehouse (SSDT). With SSDT, you can build, manage, diagnose, and refactor databases. You can work directly with a database project, an on-premises or off-premises connected database instance, or both. Use the Visual Studio Installer to install the workload for data storage and processing.

- **Debug, test, and improve your code:** You should run the code you've written after you've finished it to look for mistakes and assess how well it works. The debugging system in Visual Studio allows you to examine code that is running in a local project, on a remote device, or in a device emulator. Check variables as you go through the code, one statement at a time. You might also design breakpoints that can only be reached in certain situations. Because the code editor itself provides debug options management capabilities, you don't need to leave your code. Visual Studio offers load and performance testing, IntelliTest, Live Unit Testing, and unit testing. Visual Studio's advanced code analysis tools can be used to find problems with design, security, and other aspects.

- **Delivering your completed application**: Using InstallShield, Windows Installer, a SharePoint site, the Microsoft Store, or any combination of these, Visual Studio includes tools for distributing your program to users or clients. The Visual Studio IDE provides access to each of these functionalities.

- **Control your source code and work with others**: You may manage your source code in Git repositories provided by several companies, including GitHub, using Visual Studio. Moreover, you can look for a server to connect to in the Azure DevOps network.

# CHAPTER TWO

# EXPLORING VISUAL STUDIO USER INTERFACE

The start window is the first item you'll see when Visual Studio opens. It offers the ability to open an already existing project or solution, clone or check out code, create a new project, or just access a folder containing some code files.

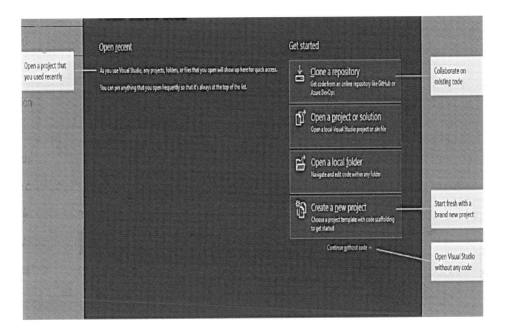

Your recent projects list will be blank if this is your first time using Visual Studio. To develop code without projects or solutions, you can open your code in Visual Studio using the Open a local folder option. If not, you can either start a brand-new project or clone an existing one from a source provider like GitHub or Azure DevOps.

The Visual Studio programming environment can also be launched without any specific project or code loaded by selecting the Continue without code option. This option can be used to attach to a process for debugging or to join a Live Sharing session. Using Esc will also close the start window and launch the IDE.

# UNDERSTANDING VISUAL STUDIO USER LAYOUT

- The style of Visual Studio Code is straightforward and simple, maximizing the amount of room allotted for the editor while providing plenty of room to navigate and access the full context of your folder or project. The UI is separated into five sections:
- **Editor:** This is where you alter your files the most. You can have as many editors open simultaneously in both vertical and horizontal orientations.
- **Side Bar:** Offers various views, such as the Explorer, to help you while you work on your project.
- **Status Bar:** Details about the active project and the edited files.
- **Activity Bar:** With the Activity Bar, which is located on the bottom left of the screen, you can switch between perspectives. When Git is activated, it also gives you more context-specific data, like the number of outgoing changes.
- **Panels:** You can display several panels below the editing zone, including ones for an integrated terminal, errors and warnings, output, and debug information. The panel can easily be relocated to the right for more vertical room.

# DIFFERENT EDITORS ARE OPEN

In both vertical and horizontal orientations, you can have an unlimited number of editors open at once. If you already have an editor open, you can open a second one while keeping the current one open in several ways:

- Alt-click on an Explorer file.
- Pressing Ctrl and splitting the active editor in half.
- In Explorer, from the context menu for a file, choose Open to the Side (Ctrl+Enter).
- Click the Split Editor button in the top right corner of the editor.
- Drag a file and drop it into any part of the editor area.
- Ctrl+Enter in the Quick Open (Ctrl+P) file list (Cmd+Enter on Mac).

Remember that any new files you open will display their contents in the editor that is presently active. When using two editors side by side, make sure the right-hand editor is active before opening the file "foo.cs" into it (by clicking inside it). By default, editors open to the right of the one that is open and working. You can override this behavior and make new editors open below the active one by specifying workbench.editor.openSideBySideDirection.

# UNDERSTANDING VISUAL STUDIO EXPLORER

Explorer is used to browse, open, and manage every file and folder in your project. You can get started straight away by opening a file or folder in Visual Studio Code because it is a file and folder-based program. After a folder has been opened in Visual Studio Code, its contents are shown in Explorer. From here, several actions are possible:

- Adding, eliminating, and renaming files and directories.
- Use drag and drop to move files and directories.
- Use the context menu to get more information about any option.

If there are no files in the explorer, Visual Studio Code will open any files you drag and drop into it from another location to transfer them.

It works nicely with other tools you might need, especially command-line tools, like Microsoft Studio Code. To run a command-line tool in the context of the folder you are now viewing, use the Open in Command Prompt or Open in Terminal options from the context menu when right-clicking the folder in VISUAL STUDIO Code.

You may also access the location of a file or folder by right-clicking on it and selecting "Reveal in Explorer," "Reveal in Finder on macOS," or "Open Containing Folder" on Linux.

# UNDERSTANDING VISUAL STUDIO MINIMAP

Using a Minimap (code outline), which gives you a high-level overview of your code, will help you explore your source code more quickly and understand it better. The minimap for a specific file is shown on the right side of the editor. By clicking or dragging the darkish region, you can quickly navigate to different sections of your file.

```js
gulp.task('clean-out-folder', common.rimraf('out'));

gulp.task('clone-vscode-website', ['clean-out-folder'], function (cb) {
    fs.mkdir('out');
    process.chdir('./out');
    git.clone(URL, function (err) {
        if (err) {
            console.log('could not clone vscode-website')
            console.log(err);
            cb(err);
        } else {
            process.chdir('./vscode-website');
            git.checkout(BRANCH, function (error) {
                console.log('checked out branch:', BRANCH);
                process.chdir('../../');
                cb(error);
            });
        }
    });
});

gulp.task('commit', function () {
    process.chdir('./out/vscode-website');
```

You can move the minimap to the left or turn it off by setting "editor.minimap.side": "left" or "editor.minimap.enabled": false in your user or workspace settings.

# UNDERSTANDING VISUAL STUDIO INDENT GUIDES

Moreover, indentation guides (vertical lines) are displayed in the above image to assist you in easily identifying matching indent levels. You can disable indented guides by setting "editor.guides.indentation" to false in your workspace or user settings.

# UNDERSTANDING VISUAL STUDIO BREADCRUMBS

Above its text, the editor has a Breadcrumbs navigation bar. It displays the current position and enables quick switching between folders, files, and symbols.

In breadcrumbs, the file path and, if the language's symbols are supported by the current file type, the symbol path up to the cursor location, are always shown. You can disable breadcrumbs using the View > Show Breadcrumbs toggle command. For more information on the breadcrumbs feature, including how to customize their appearance, see the Code Navigation article's Breadcrumbs section.

# VISUAL STUDIO ADVANCED TREE NAVIGATION

You can filter the files that are now visible in File Explorer. While keeping the focus on the File Explorer, press Ctrl/Cmd+F to open the tree find control, then type a section of the file name you want to match. The top-right Find control in the File Explorer will show what you typed and highlight any matching file names. By selecting the Filter button, you can choose between the two modes of highlighting and filtering. By hitting DownArrow, you can switch between matching elements and concentrate on the first matched element. As it is available for all tree views, feel free to test out this navigation capability in other Visual Studio Code programs.

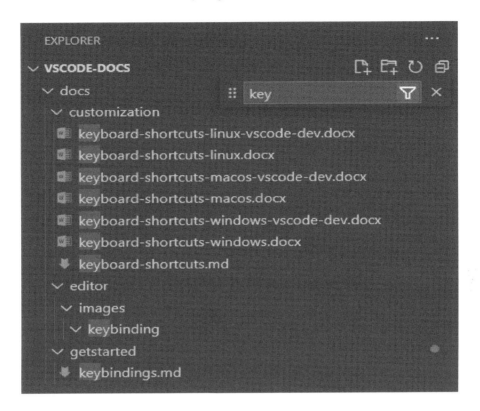

# UNDERSTANDING VISUAL STUDIO OUTLINE VIEW

The Outline view has its section at the bottom of the File Explorer. When magnified, it will show the active editor's symbol tree.

The Outline view offers a range of Sort By options in addition to supporting the common open gestures. Tracking the cursor is optional. Moreover, there is an input field that does symbol searches or filters as you type. The Outline view also shows faults and warnings, enabling you to easily pinpoint the location of a problem.

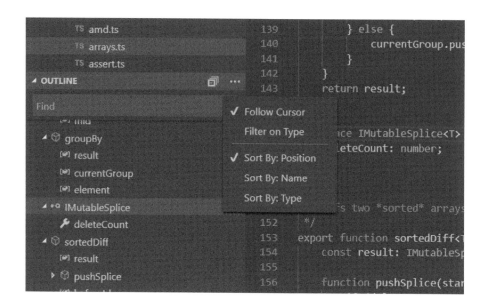

The data derived by the installed extensions you have for different file kinds is what the display for symbols is dependent on. For instance, the built-in Markdown support returns the Markdown header hierarchy when the symbols of a Markdown file are requested.

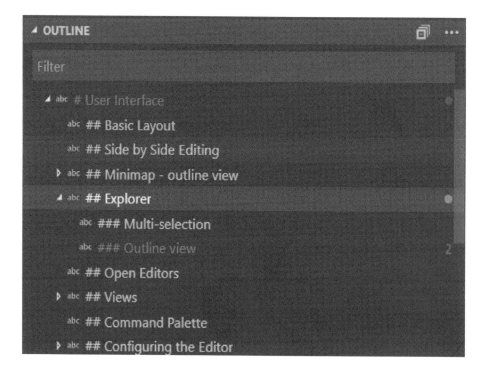

Many settings (all of which are enabled by default) allow you to enable/disable icons and control how errors and warnings are shown in the Outline view.

- **outline.icons**: Use icons to toggle the rendering of outline elements.
- **outline.problems.enabled**: Display outline element errors and warnings.
- **outline.problems.badges**: Choose between utilizing errors and warnings as badges.
- **outline.problems.colors**: Activate or deactivate the use of colored errors and warnings.

# VISUAL STUDIO OPEN EDITORS

At the top of the Explorer is the view OPEN EDITORS. Below is a list of the currently open files or previews. These are the active Visual Studio Code files that you had previously accessed. For example, a file will show up in the OPEN EDITORS view if you:

- Do a file modification.
- Click the header of a file twice.
- In Explorer, click twice on a file.
- Access a file that isn't in the currently open folder.

In Visual Studio Code, activating an item in the OPEN EDITORS window is as simple as clicking it. When you're done with your assignment, you can either use the View: Close All Editors or View: Close All Editors in Group actions to remove all files at once, or you can remove each file individually from the OPEN EDITORS view.

# UNDERSTANDING VIEWS

The File Explorer is one of the Views available in Visual Studio Code. Views are accessible for:

- **Search**: Allows you to perform a complete search and replace across all of your open folders.
- **Source control**: Visual Studio Code by default includes Git source control.
- **Run**: In Visual Studio Code's Run and Debug View, variables, call stacks, and breakpoints are shown.
- **Extensions**: Visual Studio Code allows you to manage and install extensions.
- Individual views: Extension-provided views.

You can open any view by selecting View > Open View.

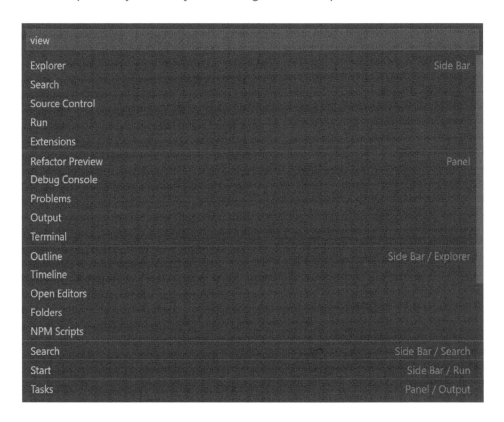

Within the main view, you may drag and drop views to change their order as well as reveal or conceal them.

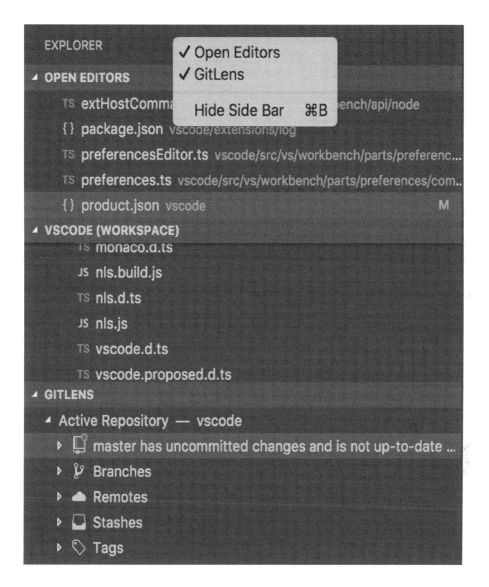

# VISUAL STUDIO ACTIVITY BAR

You may swiftly switch between Views using the left-hand Activity Bar. Views can also be completely removed or rearranged by dragging and dropping them on the Activity Bar (right-click Hide from Activity Bar).

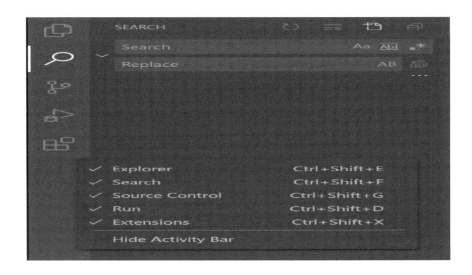

# VISUAL STUDIO COMMAND PALETTE

The keyboard provides equal access to Visual Studio Code. The key combination that opens the Command Palette, Ctrl+Shift+P, is the most crucial to remember. You may access all of Visual Studio Code's features from this point, including keyboard shortcuts for the most often operations.

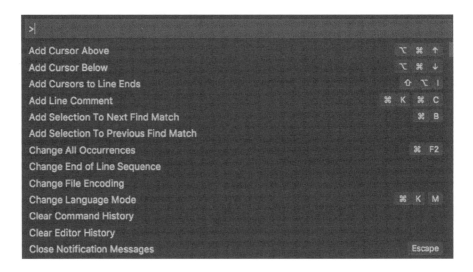

The Command Palette provides access to numerous commands. You can access files, run editor commands, look up symbols, and view a file summary all from the same interactive window. Observations are as follows:

- By inputting the name of any file or symbol, you can go to it with Ctrl+P.
- The latest group of opened files will cycle through when you press Ctrl+Tab.
- Pressing Ctrl+Shift+P will bring up the editor's commands immediately.
- By pressing Ctrl+Shift+O, you can go to a specific symbol in a file.
- By using Ctrl+G, you can navigate to a specific line in a file.

By entering "?" in the input field, you can get a list of the available commands to run from this location:

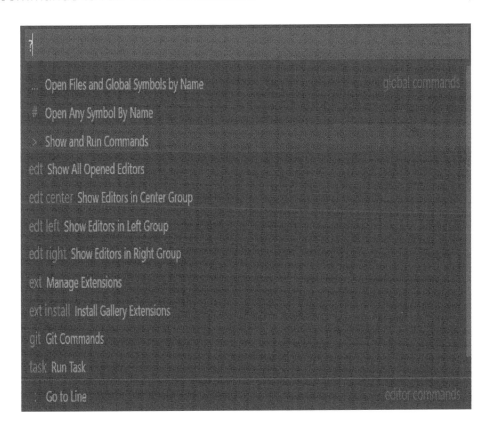

# CONFIGURING YOUR VISUAL STUDIO EDITOR

By entering "?" in the input field, you can get a list of the available commands to run from this location:

## How to Hide the Menu Bar

On Windows and Linux, the Menu Bar can be hidden by making changes to the settings box. changing menuBarVisibility's default value. With just one Alt keystroke, the Menu Bar can be brought back into Toggle mode.

On Windows and Linux, the Menu Bar can also be hidden using the View > Toggle Menu Bar command. While using this command, the window is set. When menuBarVisibility was changed from classic to compact, the Menu Bar was moved inside the Activity Bar. To reset the Menu Bar to its default state, use the View > Toggle Menu Bar command once more.

## Visual Studio Settings

The majority of editor configurations are stored in settings that can be directly changed. Options can be modified worldwide through user preferences or specifically for a project or folder through workspace preferences. A settings.json file contains the settings' values.

• Choose File > Preferences > Settings (or press Ctrl+,) to make changes to the user settings.json file.

• Selecting the WORKSPACE SETTINGS tab will allow you to edit the workspace settings.json file.

Users of macOS should be aware that the Preferences menu is located in Code, not File. For example, Code>Preferences>Settings.

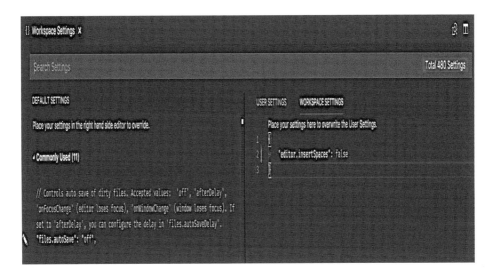

Your default settings for Visual Studio Code are available for editing in the left pane. The right is used to display json. You can rapidly filter settings in the Default Settings using the search box above. To the editable settings, copy a setting. By choosing the edit icon to the left of the option, you may view JSON on the right. The edit icon menu of settings that have a predetermined range of values allows you to choose a value. Use Ctrl+S to save changes you've made to your preferences. The changes will take effect straight now.

The distribution of team-wide project-specific options will be aided by workspace settings, which will take precedence over user settings.

# UNDERSTANDING ZEN MODE

By making the editor layout full screen, centering it, and removing everything UI other than the editor, Zen Mode helps you focus on your coding (no Activity Bar, Status Bar, Side Bar, or Panel). Activate Zen mode by using Ctrl+K on the keyboard, the View menu, or the Command Palette. By pressing the double Esc key, Zen Mode can be ended. To stop the full-screen transition, use ZenMode.fullScreen. Zen Mode's options include zenMode.hideStatusBar, zenMode.hideTabs, zenMode.fullScreen, zenMode.restore, and zenMode.centerLayout.

# UNDERSTANDING CENTERED EDITOR LAYOUT

With a centered editor layout, you may center align the editor area. This is useful when using a single editor on a big monitor. You can alter the size of the view using the side sashes (hold down the Alt key to independently move the sashes).

# UNDERSTANDING VISUAL STUDIO TABS

Open objects with Tabs are shown in the title section above the editor in Visual Studio Code (tabbed headings). When a file is opened just for that file, a new Tab is added.

With the use of tabs, you can rapidly switch between things, and you may reorder them using drag and drop.

When the number of open items exceeds the size restriction of the title area, you can display a dropdown list of tabbed items by using the Display Opened Editors command (available through the... More button). If you don't want to use Tabs, you can turn them off by setting workbench.editor.showTabs to false.

*"workbench.editor.showTabs": false*

# UNDERSTANDING TAB ORDERING

Instead of having new Tabs automatically positioned to the right of existing Tabs, you may specify where you'd like them to appear by using the workbench.editor.openPositioning property.

For example, you might prefer that new tabbed items appear on the left:

*"workbench.editor.openPositioning": "left"*

# UNDERSTANDING PREVIEW MODE

When you single-click or pick a file in Explorer and it is shown in preview mode, an existing Tab is reused. This is useful if you want to explore files quickly without having to open each one in a new tab. As you start editing a file or when you double-click it to open it in Explorer, a new Tab is opened just for that file.

The Tab title's italicized Tab heading denotes preview mode:

These settings will let you decide whether or not to constantly open a new Tab instead of using preview mode:

- The *workbench.editor.enablePreview* property, which enables or disables preview editors worldwide.
- When editors are opened from Quick Open, you can enable or disable the preview by using the *workbench.editor.enablePreviewFromQuickOpen* setting.

# UNDERSTANDING VISUAL STUDIO EDITOR GROUPS

When you divide an editor, a new zone that can accommodate several objects is created (using the Split Editor or Open to the Side commands). You can open as many editor parts simultaneously in both vertical and horizontal directions. You can see the following in the Open Editors column at the top of the Explorer view:

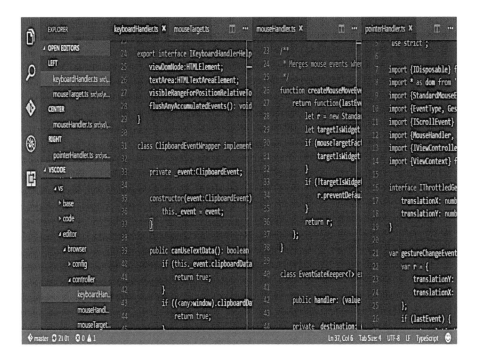

You may quickly dismiss entire groups, move specific Tabs between groups, and drag & drop editor groups on the workbench (Close All).

It's important to note that Visual Studio Code employs editor groups whether or not Tabs are enabled. In the absence of tabs, editor groups are just a stack of the open items you have, with the most recent item selected being visible in the editor pane.

# UNDERSTANDING VISUAL STUDIO GRID EDITOR LAYOUT

Editor groups are frequently shown by default in vertical columns (for example when you split an editor to open it to the side). Editor groups can be easily organized both vertically and horizontally in any layout:

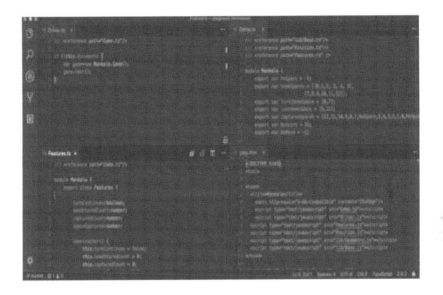

Flexible layouts can be accommodated by creating empty editor groups. You can override the default behavior of closing the final editor of an editor group and also closing the group as a whole by using the new setting workbench.editor.closeEmptyGroups: false.

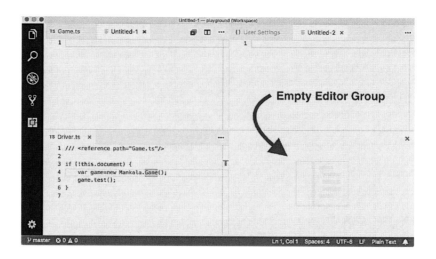

There is a predetermined list of editor layouts available under the new View > Editor Layout menu item.

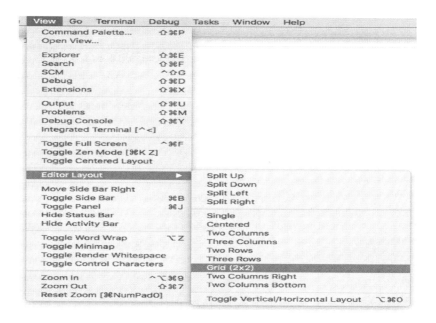

Editors that open to the side of the active editor by default do so to the right, as is the case when using the Split Editor action on the editor toolbar. Workbench.editor's new setting should be configured. If you want to open editors below the one that is now active, use openSideBySideDirection: down.

The layout of the editor can be changed using a variety of keyboard shortcuts, but if you'd prefer to use the mouse, dragging and dropping will quickly split the editor into any direction.

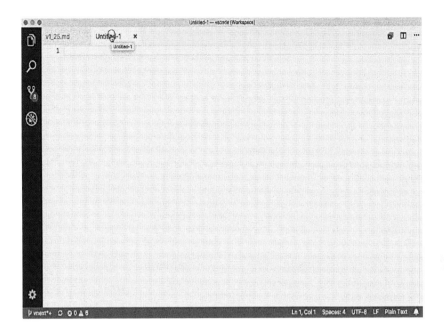

It should be noticed that when you hit and hold the Alt key while hovering over an editor, the toolbar action to split it will offer to split to the opposite orientation. This is an efficient approach to divide to the right or bottom.

# UNDERSTANDING VISUAL STUDIO WINDOW MANAGEMENT

With Visual Studio Code, some options control how windows (instances) should open or resume in between sessions. The settings window's possible values are default, on, and off. Window.openFilesInNewWindow and openFoldersInNewWindow allow you to control whether files or folders open in a new window or in the currently active window.

If left to default, we will decide whether or not to reuse a window based on the context of the open request. Turning something on or off will ensure that it behaves consistently. For example, if you want a file or folder you choose from the File menu to always open in a new window, turn this on.

Remember that in certain conditions, this setting might still not be respected (for instance, when using the command-line options -new-window or -reuse-window).

The window instructs Visual Studio Code on how to restore the windows that were open during a prior session. Windows restores a parameter. Visual Studio Code will automatically restore all of the windows you worked on during your last session (setting>all). Set this option to none to always start Visual Studio Code with a blank window, which will stop any windows from opening again. Choose either one to only restore windows with open folders or one to restore the most recently used window.

## UNDERSTANDING COLOR THEMES

You can change the colors in the Visual Studio Code user interface using color themes to match your style and working environment.

# Selecting the Color Theme

- In Visual Studio Code, select File, Choose Preferences, Choose Theme, then Color Theme to display the Color Theme selector. (On macOS, go to Code, Choose Preferences, Theme, then Color Theme).
- The picker can also be shown by pressing the keyboard shortcuts Ctrl+K and Ctrl+T.
- To preview the theme's colors, use the cursor keys.
- Click Enter after selecting the desired theme.

Your user settings (keyboard shortcut Ctrl+,) contain the active color theme.

The theme is saved in your user settings and automatically applied to all workspaces. It is also possible to create a theme specifically for a given workstation. To do this, configure a theme in the Workspace settings.

# Auto Switch Based on OS Color Scheme

Both Windows and macOS offer light and dark color palettes. A feature called autoDetectColorScheme instructs Visual Studio Code to monitor modifications to the OS's color scheme and switch to a compatible theme as needed.

You can customize the themes that are used when a color scheme changes by setting your favorite bright, dark, and high-contrast themes with the following parameters:

- The default value for workbench.preferredLightColorTheme is "Default Light+."
- The default value for *workbench.preferredDarkColorTheme* is "Default Dark+."
- "Default High Contrast" is the default value for *workbench.preferredHighContrastColorTheme*.
- "Default High Contrast Light" is the default value for *workbench.preferredHighContrastLightColorTheme*.

## Customizing a Color Theme

The workbench.colorCustomizations and editor.tokenColorCustomizations user settings allow you to modify your active color theme.

Use workbench.colorCustomizations to customize the colors of various Visual Studio Code UI elements, including lists & trees (File Explorer, recommendations widget), diff editor, Activity Bar, notifications, scroll bar, split view, buttons, and more.

When setting workbench.colorCustomizations values, you can utilize IntelliSense or consult the Theme Color Guide for a list of all colors that can be customized. The following syntax should be used if you want to solely customize one theme:

```
"workbench.colorCustomizations": {
  "[Monokai]": {
    "sideBar.background": "#347890"
  }
}
```

# UNDERSTANDING VISUAL STUDIO USER AND WORKSPACE SETTINGS

Visual Studio Code has several settings that you can adjust to your preferences. The editor, user interface, and functional behavior of Visual Studio Code can all be altered using the available settings.

Several scopes are available for settings in Visual Studio Code. There are at least two of the following scopes visible when you launch a workspace:

- **User Settings**: Options that are global to every open instance of Visual Studio Code.
- **Workspace Settings**: Preset options that only take effect when you access your workspace.

## How to Set your Editor

The Settings editor lets you review and modify user settings for Visual Studio Code. To open the Settings editor, use the menu command found in Visual Studio Code:

- Choose File, choose Preferences, then Settings on Windows or Linux.
- Choose Code, select Preferences, then Settings on MacOS.

Preferences: The Settings editor can be accessed through the Command Palette (Ctrl+Shift+P) or by using the keyboard shortcut (Ctrl+,).

When you use the Settings editor, you can search for and locate the choices you require. The Search bar will display and highlight the settings that match your criteria while filtering out any that do not when you use it to search. This makes setting discovery quick and easy.

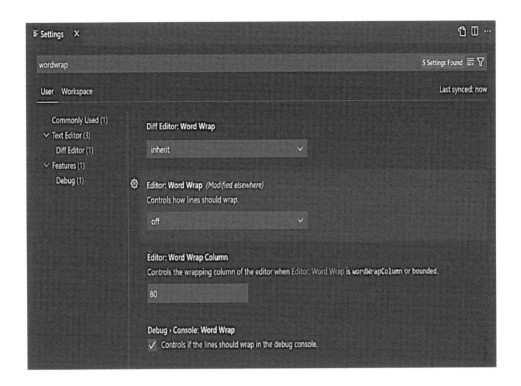

The Side Bar location and file icon theme have been modified in the example below.

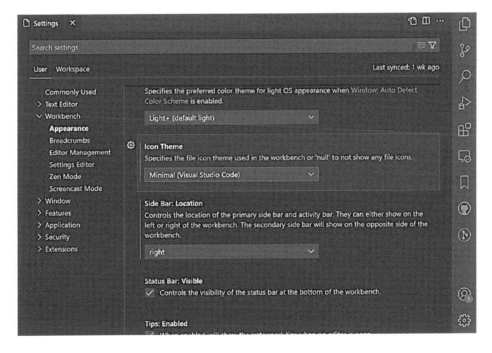

As you alter the parameters, Visual Studio Code updates them. Modified settings are identified by a blue line, just as edited lines in the editor.

You can copy the setting's ID or JSON name-value pair, as well as return the setting to its default value, from the context menu that appears when you click the gear icon and select More Actions or when you press Shift+F9.

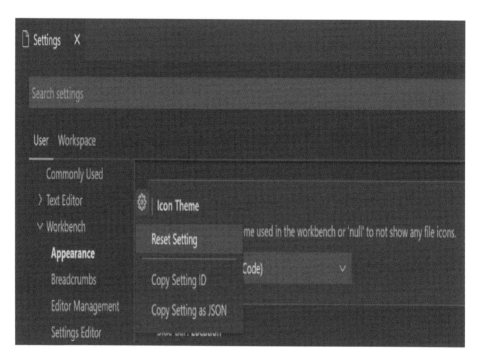

## Editing Settings

Each set has a checkbox, input, or dropdown for editing. To alter the settings, either edit the text or choose the desired option.

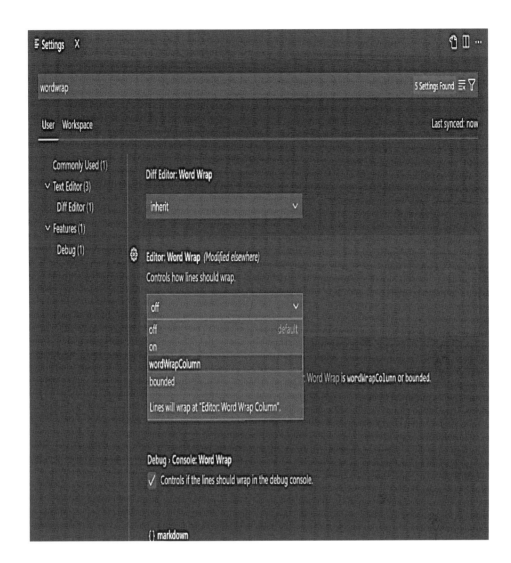

# UNDERSTANDING GROUPS SETTINGS

The settings are organized into groups for easy navigation. At the top, there is a Frequently Used group that displays the most used customizations. By choosing Source Control from the tree view, the settings for Source Control are brought into focus below.

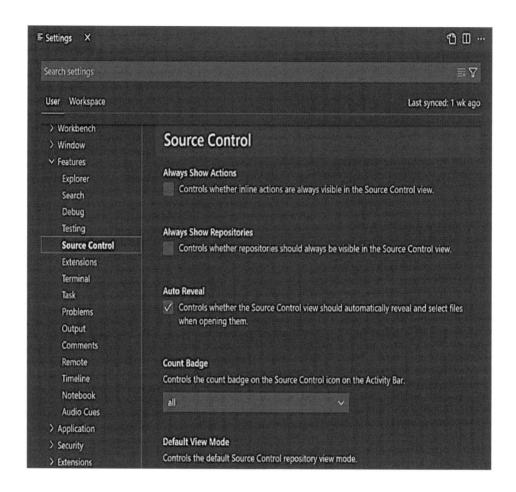

It should be noted that extensions for Visual Studio Code can also add their unique settings, and those settings will be displayed in an Extensions section.

## Changing a Setting

Let's hide the Activity Bar using Visual Studio Code as an example. There are many icons for different views, including the File Explorer, Search, Source Control, and Extensions, in the wide left border known as the "Activity Bar." You might wish to hide the Activity Bar to give the editor a bit more room or you prefer to open views via the View menu or Command Palette.

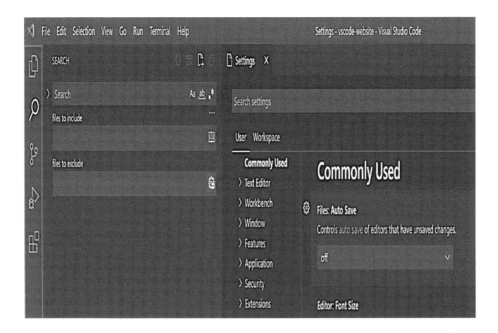

Type "activity" into the search box in the Settings Editor's search window (Ctrl+,). There should be at least five options visible.

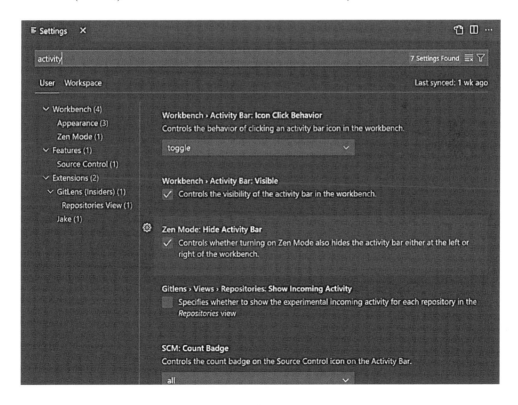

You can further limit the scope to those options in the Appearance group beneath the table of contents on the left. Currently, there should only be three choices.

Now, the Workbench > Activity Bar: Visible setting can be checked or unchecked to show or hide the Activity Bar. After you have changed the setting value from its default value, you will notice a blue line to the left.

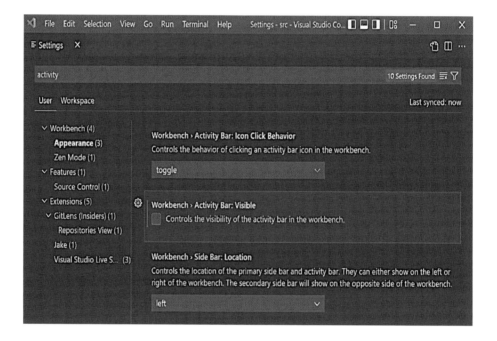

You can always reset a setting to its default value by highlighting a setting to display the gear icon, clicking on the gear icon, and then selecting the Reset Setting option.

# UNDERSTANDING SETTINGS EDITOR FILTERS

The Settings editor Search box has some filters to help manage your settings easier. To the right of the search bar is a filter button with a funnel icon that provides numerous options for quickly adding a filter.

# UNDERSTANDING MODIFIED SETTINGS

You can check which settings you've changed using the @modified filter in the Search field. It will be included in this filter if a setting's value differs from the default value or if it is explicitly set in the pertinent settings JSON file. The editor may behave differently than you would anticipate due to an unintentional configuration, so this filter can be useful if you can't remember if you configured a setting or if it happened accidentally.

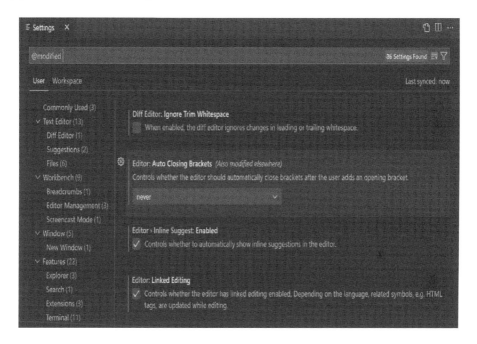

# UNDERSTANDING VISUAL STUDIO TERMINAL WINDOW

The Developer Command Prompt and Developer PowerShell shells are available on a terminal that is already included in Visual Studio as of version 2019. There can be multiple open windows in each shell's tabs. The Visual Studio terminal is built on Windows Terminal as its base. In Visual Studio, select View > Terminal to open the terminal.

When you launch Visual Studio as a standalone application or in the Terminal window if you have a solution loaded, one of the developer shells opens to the directory of your current solution. This behavior makes it easy to run commands on the solution or its projects.

Both shells already have specific environment variables set up to make using command-line programming tools easier. When opening one of these shells, you can enter the commands for some tools without being aware of their locations.

Visual Studio Code offers an integrated terminal that launches at the top of your workspace and is fully functional. It enables editor integration to allow features like links and error detection. Get the terminal going by:

- Use the keyboard shortcut Ctrl+' to switch the terminal panel.
- Use the Ctrl+Shift+' keyboard shortcut to launch a new terminal.
- Choose View > Terminal and Terminal > Build Terminal from the menu.
- Employ the Command Palette's View Toggle Terminal command (Ctrl+Shift+P).

Remember to launch an external terminal using the Ctrl+Shift+C keyboard shortcut if you prefer to work outside of Visual Studio Code.

# UNDERSTANDING TERMINAL SHELLS

Although it can use any shell installed on your computer, the integrated terminal uses the default shell from your system defaults. The dropdown menu for terminal profiles includes shell identification and display.

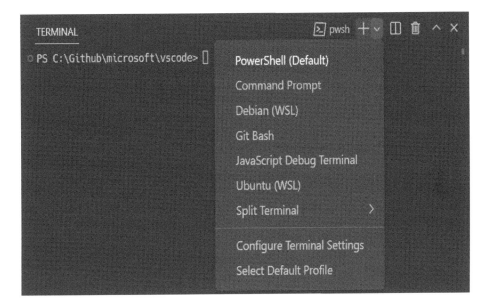

# UNDERSTANDING TERMINALS MANAGEMENT

The terminal tabs user interface is located on the right side of the terminal screen. Each terminal's name, icon, color, and group decoration are listed in its entry, if there is one.

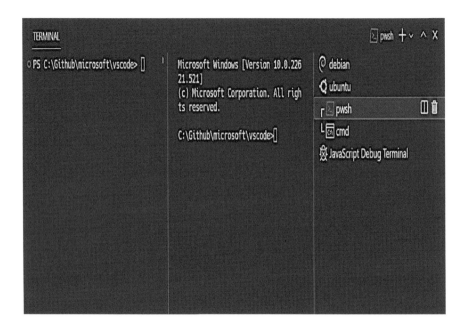

To add new terminal instances, use the Ctrl+Shift+' command, the Plus icon in the top-right corner of the TERMINAL panel, or the terminal drop-down menu. This operation adds a new tab to the list of tabs for that terminal.

The Terminal can be used to get rid of instances: Kill the Active Terminal Instance command, the right-click context menu, selecting an item on a tab and pressing Delete, hovering over a tab and selecting the Trash Can button, and any of the aforementioned techniques.

To switch between terminal groups, press Ctrl+PageUp for focus prior and Ctrl+PageDown for focus next. Icons could appear to the right of the terminal title on the tab label as the status of the terminal changes.

# UNDERSTANDING GROUPS OR SPLIT PANES

Splitting a terminal creates a set of terminals that can be arranged next to one another:

- Clicking the inline split button while hovering.

- To right-click the menu, select Split menu from the context menus.
- Press Alt and select one tab, the + button, or the + sign on the terminal panel.
- Using the shortcut Ctrl+Shift+5.

The new terminal's working directory is dependent on the *terminal.integrated.* Setting for *splitCwd*. Focus the preceding or subsequent panes of a set of terminals by pressing Alt+Left or Alt+Right, respectively.

Drag and drop operations can be used to reorder the tabs in the list. Drag a tab into the main terminal area to move a terminal from one group to another. To add a terminal to a group, use the right-click context menu or the Terminal: Unsplit Terminal command from the Command Palette.

# UNDERSTANDING THE EDITOR AREA TERMINALS

The Terminal commands In the editor area and terminal, create a new terminal: You can generate terminals in the editor area, commonly known as terminal editors, by clicking Create New Terminal in Editor Area to the Side or by dragging a terminal from the terminal view into the editor area.

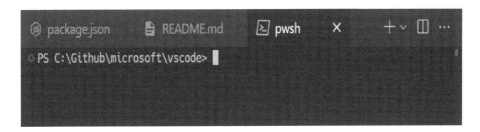

Terminal editors are the best choice if you want to set up a complex workbench with terminals in two different dimensions or on either side of an editor. Underneath a stack of file editors to the right is a selection of PowerShell and WSL terminals.

Integrated within the terminal. The default terminal location can be changed by the defaultLocation parameter to either the view or editor areas.

# UNDERSTANDING VISUAL STUDIO OUTPUT WINDOW

Status messages for various features of the integrated development environment are displayed in the Output pane (IDE). Use Ctrl+Alt+O to bring up the Output window, or select View > Output from the menu bar.

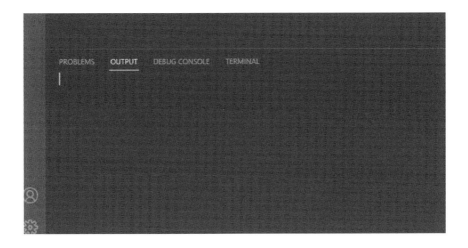

# UNDERSTANDING VISUAL STUDIO SOURCE CONTROL

An overview of the number of modifications you presently have in your repository is always displayed via the Source Control icon in the Activity Bar on the left. Choosing the icon will provide information about the CHANGES, STAGED CHANGES, and MERGE CHANGES in your current repository.

By clicking on each item, you can see the precise text changes that were made to each file. Please feel free to make unstaged adjustments to the file using the editor on the right. Other repository status indicators may be found in the bottom-left corner of Visual Studio Code, including the current branch, unclean indications, and the number of incoming and outgoing commits for the current branch. You can check out any branch in your repository by picking the Git reference from the list after clicking that status signal.

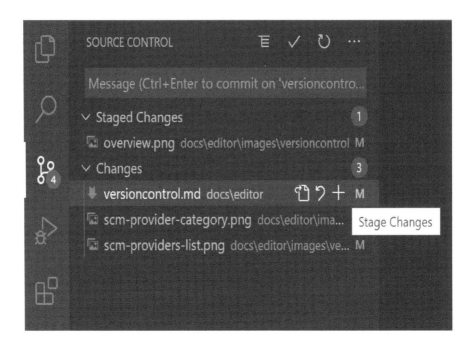

# UNDERSTANDING DEBUG CONSOLE

You can give the debug engine commands using the debug console. You can also view engine output and the outcomes of your commands with this tool.

The Run and Debug view contains a top bar with debugging commands and setup options, and it displays all information about running and debugging. VISUAL STUDIO Code displays the Run start view if running and debugging are not yet setup (no launch.json has been produced).

# UNDERSTANDING DEBUGGING

One of Visual Studio Code's unique characteristics is the superb debugging tools it provides. Using the built-in debugger in Microsoft Studio Code will speed up the edit, compile, and debug loop.

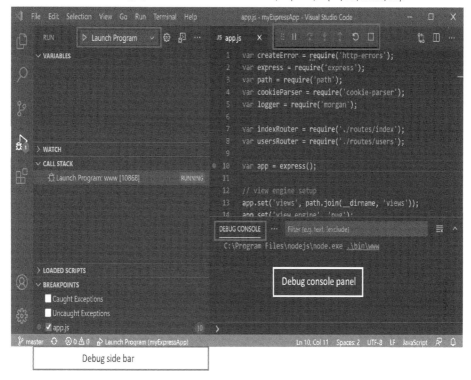

Start debugging

Pause, step over, step in/out, restart, stop

Debug console panel

Debug side bar

# UNDERSTANDING DEBUGGER EXTENSIONS

JavaScript, TypeScript, and any other language that has been translated to JavaScript may all be debugged with Microsoft Studio Code. Moreover, it offers built-in Node.js runtime debugging support.

You may debug C#, Python, Ruby, Go, PowerShell, and many more programming languages and runtimes by searching for Debuggers extensions in the Visual Studio Code Marketplace or by selecting Install Additional Debuggers from the top-level Run menu.

To access the Run and Debug view in Visual Studio Code, select the icon for Run and Debug in the Activity Bar on the side. Another potential keyboard shortcut is Ctrl+Shift+D.

The Run and Debug view shows all running and debugging-related information and has a top bar with debugging commands and configuration options. If running and debugging is not yet configured, Visual Studio Code shows the Run start view during launch. It has generated json.

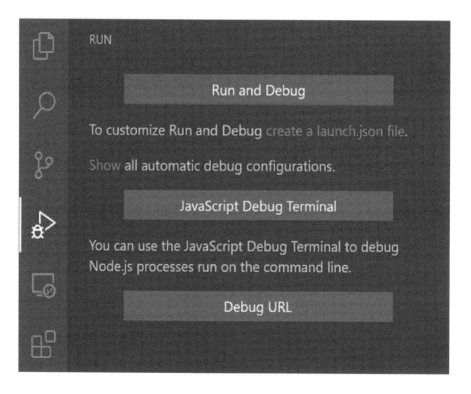

# CHAPTER THREE

# UNDERSTANDING FILES, FOLDERS, AND PROJECT EXPLORER

Explorer is used to browse, open, and manage every file and folder in your project. You can get started straight away by opening a file or folder in Visual Studio Code because it is a file and folder-based program.

After a folder has been opened in Visual Studio Code, its contents are shown in Explorer. From here, you can carry out several tasks, including.

- Creating, deleting, and renaming files and directories.
- Use drag and drop to move files and directories.
- Use the context menu to get more information about any option.

Remember that if Explorer is empty, you can copy files by dragging and dropping them from somewhere into Explorer, and Visual Studio Code will open them in its place.

## UNDERSTANDING VISUAL STUDIO PROJECT

An MSBuild build system is used to construct a Visual Studio project, which is a collection of code files and assets like icons, graphics, and so forth. The ideal build system to utilize for Windows-specific apps is MSBuild, which is native to Visual Studio.

# UNDERSTANDING VISUAL STUDIO FILES

With Visual Studio projects for traditional desktop programs, files are linked. Your project's actual files will vary depending on the project type and wizard choices you choose.

# UNDERSTANDING FOLDERS

On a computer, a folder also known as a directory is a place where files, other folders, and shortcuts are kept. The manila folders used in offices to keep documents and reports serve as an effective comparison. A subfolder is a folder that is housed within another folder.

A folder is similar to a master file in that it may hold both files and other folders. A file's precise location is known as its path, which includes all of the folders heading there. Using the filename as an example. For simple navigation, Visual Studio files and projects are kept in a folder. Create the following folders, files, and projects.

- Decide where you want your folder to be located.
- Make a new selection with a right-click in that area.
- Choose the appropriate folder and enter the folder name.
- Get Visual Studio launching.
- Choose the open folder when you click on the file.
- The folder will open after you locate it, select it, and click Choose Folder.

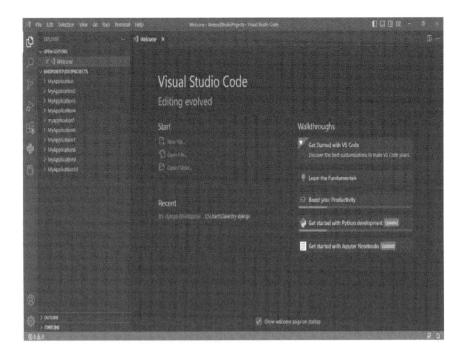

- Now that you have clicked Create File, you can begin adding files to your folder.
- Press the Enter key after entering the file's name and extension.
- Write your code after clicking to create the file.

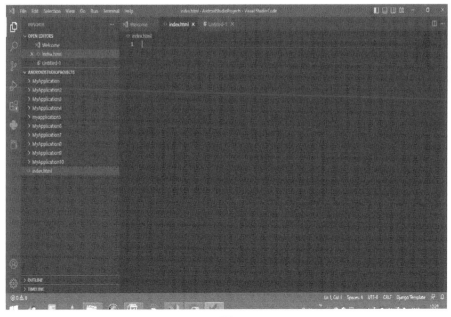

- The code file that was saved now serves as your project.

# UNDERSTANDING DECORATIONS IN VISUAL STUDIO

To adorn sections of code, the Decorations API was added to Visual Studio Code. It enables you to choose text regions in an editor and embellish them with a subset of CSS characteristics. It adds a visual component to how you can read your code in Visual Studio Code rather than altering the code itself. The extension community has used decorations widely for better views.

# UNDERSTANDING WORKSPACES

A "workspace" in Visual Studio Code is a group of one or more folders that are open in a Visual Studio Code window (instance). The workspace will typically be a single folder that has been opened, but depending on your development workflow, you may be able to use Multi-root workspaces, a sophisticated option. The idea of a workspace gives Visual Studio Code the ability to:

- Set preferences that only apply to one or more specified folders and not others.
- Maintain configurations for task and debugger launches that are unique to that workspace.
- Save and retrieve UI state relevant to that workspace (for example, the files that are opened).
- Just for that workspace, selectively enable or disable extensions.

In the documentation, problems, and community conversations for Visual Studio Code, the terms "folder" and "workspace" may be interchanged. Consider a workspace as the hub of a project that contains additional Visual Studio Code information and features.

Visual Studio Code can also be launched without a workspace. For instance, you won't be within a workspace when you choose a file from your platform's File menu to start a new Visual Studio Code window. Although certain Visual Studio Code features are limited in this mode, text files can still be opened and edited.

## How Visual Studio Code Workspace Can Be Opened

The simplest method to launch a workspace is to use the File menu and select one of the openable folder entries. When starting Visual Studio Code from a terminal, an alternative is to pass the path to a folder as the first argument to the code command.

## Understanding Workspace Settings

You can alter settings for the active workspace by using workspace settings, which always take precedence over global user settings. They are physically saved in a JSON file, depending on whether you opened a folder as a workspace or a.code-workspace file. See the settings page for a detailed explanation of setting scopes and where to find them in files.

## The Single-folder Workspace Settings

The file VisualStudiocode/settings.json is where workspace preferences are recorded when a folder is accessed as a workspace. The Settings editor is displayed below when a folder is selected as the workspace.

## The Multi-root Workspace Settings

When you open a .code-workspace as a workspace, all workspace settings will be added to the .code-workspace file.

In addition to the ability to customize settings per root folder, the Settings editor will offer a third option scope named Folder Settings. The Settings editor displays as seen below when a multi-root workspace is opened.

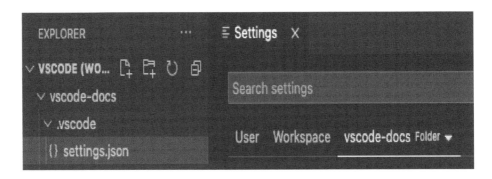

Remember that parameters configured per folder will take precedence over choices defined in the .code-workspace.

# UNDERSTANDING SEARCH

You may rapidly search through all of the files in the currently opened folder in Visual Studio Code. To search, use Ctrl+Shift+F and type your phrase. The search term-containing files in which the results are gathered along with a description of the hits in each file's location. To

82

obtain a preview of every hit contained in a file, expand the file. then click once to open the editor by selecting one of the hits.

By selecting the ellipsis (Toggle Search Details) next to the search field on the right (or using Ctrl+Shift+J), you may set up advanced search parameters. More fields for configuring the search will appear as a result.

## The Advanced Search Options

You can enter patterns to include or omit from the search in the two input boxes that are located beneath the search box. If you type an example, every folder and file with that name in the workspace will match. The folder example/ at the top level of your workspace, which is used to divide up many patterns, will be matched if you type ./example. Forward slashes are required in paths.

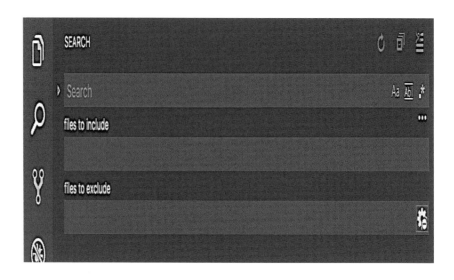

You can also use glob syntax:

- To match one character in a path segment, use ?, and use * to match on zero or more characters.
- ** to match a single path segment or any number of them, even none.
- To group conditions (for instance, "**/*.html," "**/*.txt" matches all HTML and text files, respectively).
- [] to specify a character range to match (example.[0-9] to match on example.0, example.1,...).
- [!...] to indicate that a specific set of characters should not match (example.[!0-9] to match on example.a and example.b but not example.0).

To decrease the number of search results that you are not interested in, Visual Studio Code automatically excludes specific folders (such as node modules). To modify these restrictions, open settings and go to the *files.exclude* and *search.exclude* sections.

Be aware that glob patterns behave differently in the search view than they do in settings like *files.exclude* and *search.exclude*. To match a folder named example in a subdirectory called folder1/example in your workspace, you must enter **/example in the settings. The ** prefix is taken for granted in the search view. The workspace folder path is always taken into consideration while evaluating the glob patterns in these settings.

Especially take note of the toggle buttons Use Exclude Settings and Ignore Files in the files to exclude the box. With the toggle, you may choose whether or not to include files that are matched by your files and/or ignored by your *.gitignore* files. settings for exclude and *search.exclude*.

To search solely within a folder, right-click on the folder in Explorer and choose to Find in Folder.

## Understanding Search and Replace

Moreover, you may search and replace among files. To make the Replace text box visible, expand the Search widget.

As you type in the Replace text box, a diff display of the pending changes will appear. You can replace every item in a single file, all the modifications in a single file, or simply one alteration using the Replace text box.

You can quickly re-use a previous search phrase by choosing Down and Up to navigate through your search term history.

Visual Studio Code additionally supports changing the case of regex matching groups while doing Search and Replace in the editor or globally. The modifiers \u\U\l, and \L are used to do this; \u and /l will upper- and lower-case a single character, respectively, while \U and \L will do the same for the remaining characters in the matching group. View the illustration below.

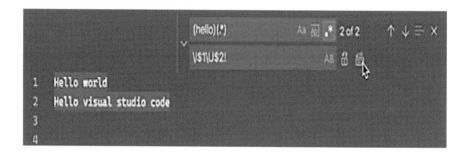

It is also possible to combine the modifiers; for example, u\u\u\u$1 will capitalize the first three letters of the group whereas l\U\$1 will lowercase the first letter while capitalizing the rest. The replacement string uses $n to denote the capture group, where n denotes the order of the capture group.

## Understanding Search Editor

With search editors, you may review workspace search results in a large editor with syntax highlighting and optional lines of the surrounding context.

Below is a search for the word "SearchEditor" with two lines of context-rich text before and after the match.

The Open Search Editor command launches an existing Search Editor. If not, a new one is made. When the New Search Editor command is invoked, a new Search Editor is always created.

One can browse the search results using the Go to Definition actions in the Search Editor, such as F12 to open the source location in the current editor group or Ctrl+K and F12 to open the location in a side editor. Moreover, users can decide whether double-clicking should instantly access the source location by setting the search.searchEditor.doubleClickBehaviour parameter.

As an alternative, you can copy your current results from a Search view to a Search Editor by using the Open New Search Editor button at the top of the Search view, the Open in editor link at the top of the results tree, or the Search Editor: Open Results in Editor command.

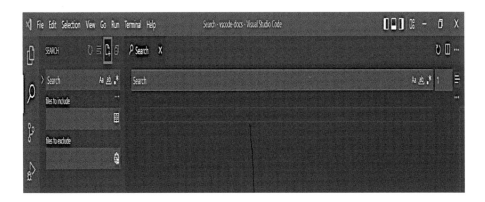

The Search Editor displayed above was opened by selecting the third button, labeled "Open New Search Editor," at the top of the Search window. The commands and arguments for the Search Editor are listed below.

- *search.action.openNewEditor:* Opens a new tab with the Search Editor open.
- *search.action.openInEditor:* Copy the current search results to a new Search Editor.
- *search.action.openNewEditorToSide:* adjoins the window you've already opened with a new one that contains the Search Editor.

To enable keybindings to customize how a new Search Editor should operate, there are two options that you may supply to the

*search.action.openNewEditor* and
*search.action.openNewEditorToSide* commands.

- *triggerSearch*: whether a search will start when a search editor is opened automatically. The default is true.
- *focusResults*: Deciding whether to focus on a search's results or the query's input. The default is true.

# UNDERSTANDING FIND AND REPLACE

In Visual Studio Code, you can quickly search and replace text in an open file. The overview ruler and minimap of the editor will highlight the search results when the Find Widget is activated by pressing Ctrl+F. If there are several matched results in the currently opened file, you can press Enter or Shift+Enter while the search input box is focused to go to the next or previous result.

# EXPLORING THE SEED SEARCH STRING FROM SELECTION

When the Find Widget is opened, the editor's selected text will automatically fill the find input box. In the absence of a selection, the word under the cursor will be entered into the input area.

By using the configuration editor, this feature can be disabled. False is the value for *find.seedSearchStringFromSelection*.

# UNDERSTANDING FIND IN SELECTION

The editor executes find operations on the whole file by default. It can also be used to run the chosen text. You can access this function by clicking the hamburger icon on the Find Widget.

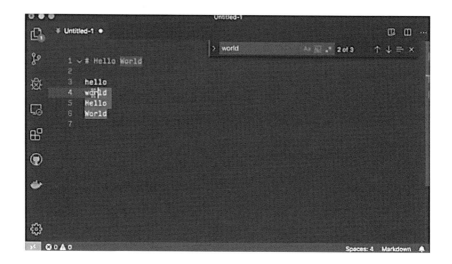

The Find Widget's default behavior can be changed by setting editor.find.autoFindInSelection to always, or you can set it to multiline to only operate on selected text when multiple lines of content are selected.

# UNDERSTANDING SOPHISTICATED FIND AND REPLACE OPTIONS

In addition, to locate and replace with plain text, the Find Widget also offers the following three sophisticated search options:

- Match Case.
- Whole-Word Match.

- Whole-Word Match.

By selecting the Preserve Case (AB) option, you can enable case-preserving in the replace input box.

# CHAPTER FOUR

# INTEGRATING WITH SOURCE CONTROL

The source control management of Visual Studio Code has integrated Git support (SCM). Numerous alternative source control providers are available as add-ons in the Visual Studio Code Marketplace.

## USING GIT

If you're just learning about Git, the git-scm website is a great place to start because it offers a well-liked online book, Getting Started lessons, and cheat sheets. The Visual Studio Code guide assumes that you are familiar with Git.

## KNOW THE FOLLOWING ABOUT GIT

- Check that Git is configured. To use these features, you must first install Git since Visual Studio Code requires that Git be installed on your machine (at least version 2.0.0).
- The Source Control icon in the Activity Bar on the left is always used to give a summary of the number of modifications you currently have in your repository. When you select the icon, details about the CHANGES, STAGED CHANGES, and MERGE CHANGES in your current repository will be displayed.
- By clicking on each item, you can see the precise text changes that were made to each file. Please be aware that the editor on the right still enables you to make unstaged changes to the file; feel free to use it.
- More repository status indicators may be found in the bottom-left corner of Visual Studio Code, including the current branch, unclean indications, and the number of incoming and outgoing commits for the current branch. You can checkout any branch

in your repository by picking the Git reference from the list after clicking that status signal.

- In the subfolder of a Git repository, Visual Studio Code can be started. Changes to files outside of the scoped directory are darkened and have a tooltip showing their position outside the current workspace, but the Git services in Visual Studio Code continue to run normally and display any changes made to files in the repository.

# WORKING WITH GITHUB IN VISUAL STUDIO CODE

A cloud-based service for storing and sharing source code is called GitHub. You may share your source code and work with others directly inside your editor by integrating GitHub with Visual Studio Code. There are other methods to communicate with GitHub, such as through their website at *https://github.com* or the Git command-line interface (CLI), but the GitHub Pull Requests and Issues extension in Visual Studio Code offers the most thorough interaction with the platform.

# THE GITHUB PULL REQUESTS AND ISSUES EXTENSION SHOULD BE INSTALLED

To begin using GitHub in Visual Studio Code, you must first install Git, create an account on GitHub, and add the GitHub Pull Requests and Issues extension. In this chapter, we'll demonstrate how to use a few of your favorite GitHub features without ever leaving Visual Studio Code. If you're not familiar with source control or want to learn more about the basic Git support offered by Visual Studio Code, you can start with Source Control.

# HOW TO BEGIN WITH GITHUB PULL REQUESTS AND PROBLEMS

After installing the GitHub Pull Requests and Issues extension, you must log in. After answering the GitHub login questions in the browser, go back to Visual Studio Code.

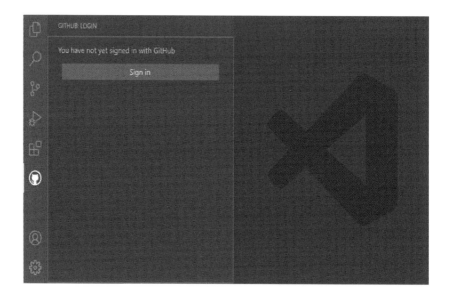

After installing the GitHub Pull Requests and Issues extension, you must log in. After answering the GitHub login questions in the browser, go back to Visual Studio Code.

## REPOSITORY SET-UP

When you don't have a folder open, you can search for and clone a GitHub repository by pressing Ctrl+Shift+P on your keyboard or the Clone Repository button in the Source Control window.

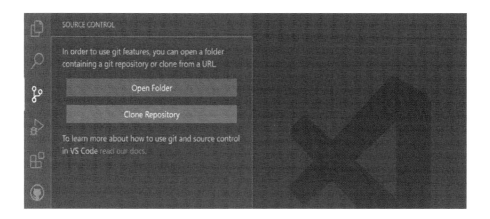

The GitHub repository selection can be filtered to help you find the repository you wish to locally clone.

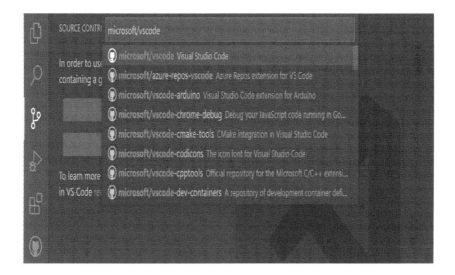

# USING AN EXISTING REPOSITORY FOR AUTHENTICITY

You enable GitHub authentication whenever you carry out a Git operation in Visual Studio Code that requires GitHub authentication, such as pushing to a repository to which you have access or cloning a private repository. Because authentication is already included in Visual Studio Code, you can easily manage your repository without installing any additional plugins. You will be requested to sign in as follows when carrying out an operation that requires a GitHub login:

Follow the directions to sign into GitHub and return to Visual Studio Code. If automatic authentication with an existing repository doesn't work, you might have to manually enter a personal access token. See Personal Access Token authentication for further information.

You can sign in to GitHub using a personal access token, an SSH key, or your username and password with two-factor authentication (2FA). Authentication to GitHub has further details and information on each option. You may browse and edit repositories on GitHub without first copying their contents to your computer by installing the GitHub Repositories extension. Further details can be found in the section below about the GitHub Repositories extension.

## UNDERSTANDING EDITOR INTEGRATION

A GitHub-style hover will appear over a user's username when they are @-mentioned in an open repository.

There is a comparable hover for the #mentioned issue numbers, whole GitHub issue URLs, and repository-specific issues.

Users can choose which issues appear in suggestions by adjusting the GitHub Issues: Queries (githubIssues.queries) parameter. The queries use the GitHub search syntax.

You may also manage which files these recommendations appear for using the settings. Ignore User Completion Trigger (GitHub Issues) and Ignore Completion Trigger (githubIssues.ignoreCompletionTrigger) (githubIssues.ignoreUserCompletionTrigger). These parameters accept an array of language IDs to determine the file formats.

# UNDERSTANDING PULL REQUESTS

You can see, manage, and make pull requests using the Pull Requests view.

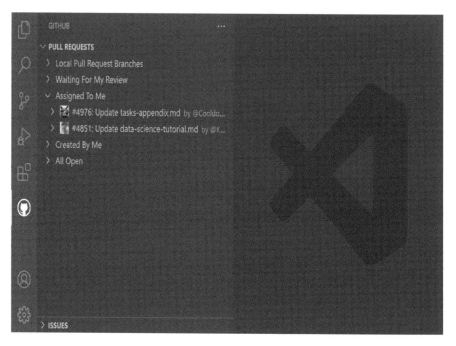

The search syntax used to display pull requests can be modified by users using the GitHub Pull Requests: Queries (githubPullRequests.queries) functionality.

```
C: > Users > Admin > Desktop > 🐍 index.py
1    "githubPullRequests.queries": [
2        {
3            "label": "Assigned To Me",
4            "query": "is:open assignee:${user}"
5        },
6
```

# HOW TO CREATE PULL REQUESTS

Once you've committed changes to your fork or branch, you can start a pull request by using the GitHub Pull Requests: Create Pull Request command or the Create Pull Request button in the Pull Requests view.

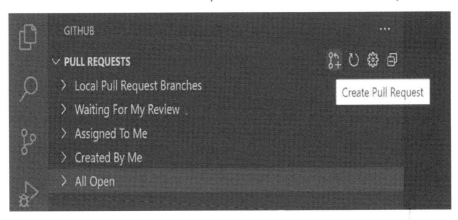

In the new New Pull Request window that will display, you may specify the repository and branch that your pull request should target as well as details like the title, description, and if it is a draft PR. If a pull request template is present in your repository, it will be used immediately as the description.

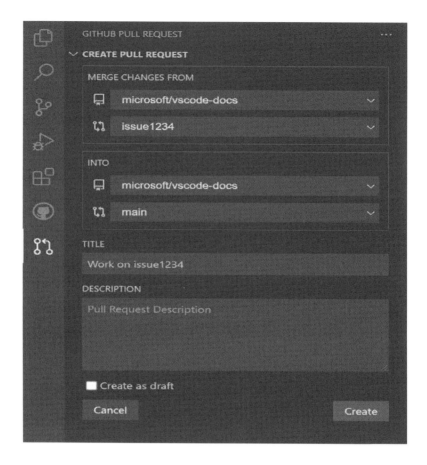

- When you choose to Create, the extension will prompt you to push your branch to a GitHub remote if you haven't previously done so and give you the option to select the proper remote.
- The New Pull Request page is currently in Review Mode. Here, you can evaluate the details of the PR, add comments, reviewers, and labels, then, when it's complete, merge the PR.
- Once the PR has been merged, you will have the option of deleting both the local branch and the remote branch.

Pull requests can be viewed in the Pull Requests page. You can add comments, assign reviewers and labels, approve, close, and merge from the pull request description.

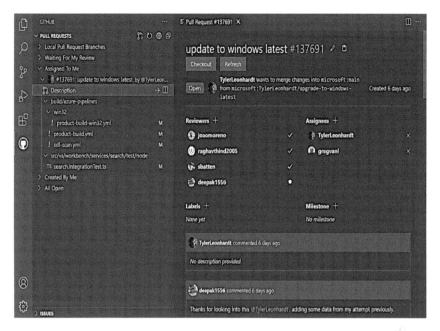

Locally checking out the pull request is also made simple by the Checkout button on the Description page. When you do this, VISUAL STUDIO Code will go into review mode, open the fork and branch of the pull request that is indicated in the status bar, and create a new Changes in Pull Request view from which you can examine the differences between all commits and the changes contained within them as well as the most recent changes. Whenever a file has comments, a diamond icon appears next to it. To view the file on disk, use the inline action Open File.

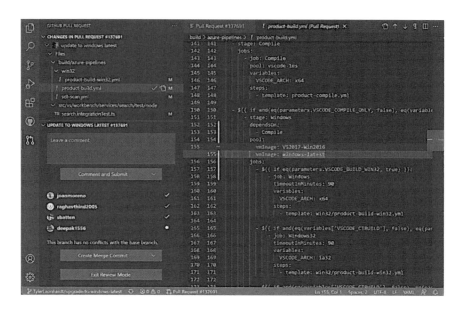

Editing, IntelliSense, and file navigation all work as expected because the diff editors from this view use the local file. You can leave feedback in the editor on these variations. Both a single comment and a comprehensive review can be added.

Once you have completed reviewing the changes, you may choose to merge the pull request or exit review mode and go back to the branch you were working on before.

# UNDERSTAND HOW TO CREATE ISSUES

You can add issues using the GitHub Issues: command or the + button in the Issues interface. The Create Issue from Selection and Create Issue from Clipboard buttons in GitHub Issues. A Code Action can also be used to generate "TODO" comments. When creating issues, you have the option of using the default description or opening an editor by clicking the pencil in the top right corner.

With the GitHub Issues: Generate Issue Triggers (githubIssues.createIssueTriggers) configuration, you can customize the Code Action trigger. Standard issue triggers include:

```
"githubIssues.createIssueTriggers": [
  "TODO",
  "todo",
  "BUG",
  "FIXME",
  "ISSUE",
  "HACK"
]
```

# WORKING ON ISSUES

Your issues are visible in the Issues view, where you may also work on them.

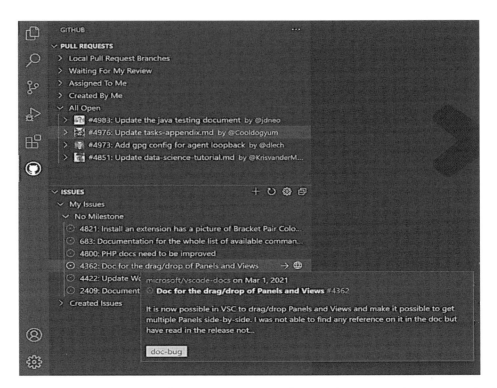

As can be seen in the Status bar in the below image, when you start working on a problem, a branch will automatically be created for you, as can be seen in the Start Working on Issue context menu option.

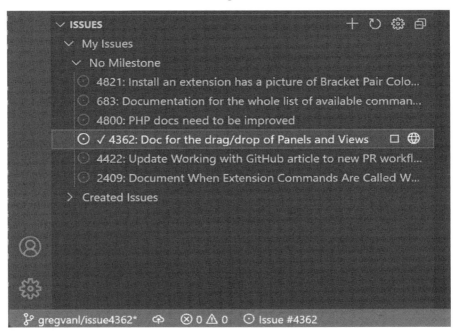

Also, the active issue is shown in the Status bar, and selecting it gives you access to some problem options, such as accessing the issue on the GitHub website and making a pull request.

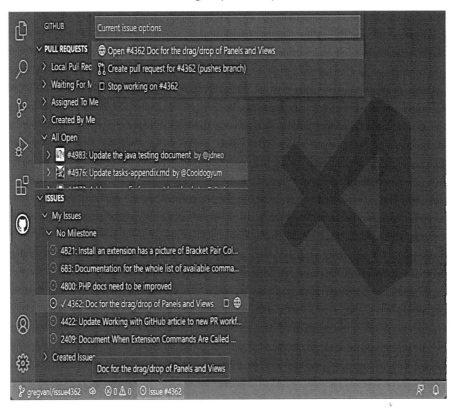

You can change the branch's name using the GitHub Issues: Issue Branch Title (githubIssues.issueBranchTitle) property. If your workflow doesn't call for it or you'd rather be prompted for a branch name each time, you may skip this step by disabling the GitHub Issues: Use Branch For Issues (githubIssues.useBranchForIssues) parameter.

Whenever you have done working on the issue and want to submit a change, the commit message input box in the Source Control view will be filled with a message. Using GitHub Issues: Working Issue Format SCM, you can alter this message (githubIssues.workingIssueFormatScm).

# UNDERSTANDING GITHUB REPOSITORIES EXTENSION

With the GitHub Repositories extension, you can quickly browse, search, edit, and commit to any remote GitHub repository from within Visual Studio Code without having to first clone it locally. This can be quick and practical in many instances where you only need to inspect the source code or make a little modification to a file or object.

## Opening a Repository

With the GitHub Repositories: Access Repository command from the Command Palette (Ctrl+Shift+P), or by clicking the Remote icon in the bottom left corner of the Status bar after installing the extension, you can access a repository.

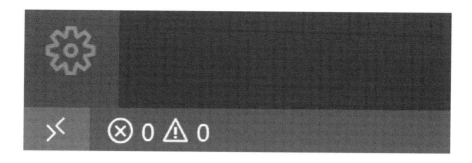

You can choose to open a repository from GitHub, a pull request from GitHub, or reconnect to an already open repository when using the Open Repository command.

While using Visual Studio Code to access GitHub, you will be prompted to log in with your GitHub account if you haven't already.

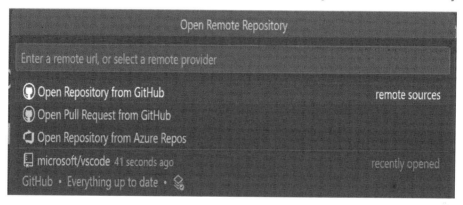

To find a repository on GitHub, you can either type in the URL directly or use the search bar. Once you have selected a repository or Pull Request, the Visual Studio Code window will reload and the repository contents will show up in the File Explorer. You may then read files (with full syntax highlighting and bracket matching), make modifications, and commit changes just like working on a local copy of a repository.

One difference between working with a local repository and utilizing the GitHub Repository extension is the ability to submit changes to the remote repository instantly, just like you would if you were using the GitHub online interface.

With the GitHub Repositories addon, you get the most recent sources from GitHub each time you access a repository or branch. As opposed to a local repository, you don't need to remember to pull to refresh.

## UNDERSTANDING SWITCHING BRANCHES

You can quickly switch branches by clicking on the branch indication in the Status bar. With the help of the GitHub Repositories addon, you can switch branches without having to save uncommitted changes. When you switch branches, the plugin remembers your modifications and applies them again.

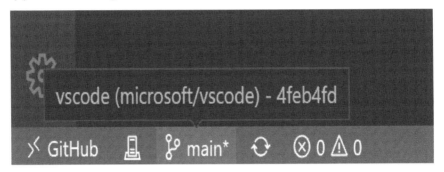

## UNDERSTANDING REMOTE EXPLORER

Remote repositories can be instantly reopened using the Remote Explorer tool located on the Activities bar. This view displays the branches and repositories that have already been opened.

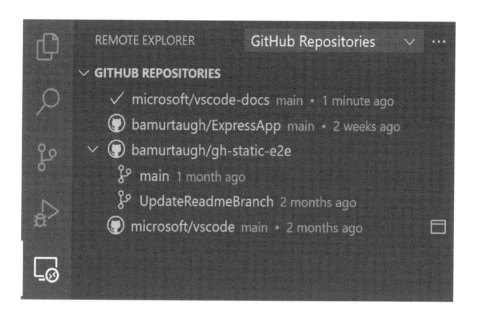

# UNDERSTANDING HOW TO CREATE PULL REQUESTS

If your workflow uses pull requests (PRs) rather than direct changes to a repository, you can create a new PR from the Source Control view. You will be prompted to create a new branch and enter a title.

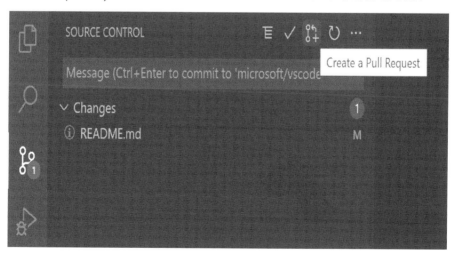

Using the preceding portions of this topic's GitHub Pull Request and Issues extension, you can evaluate, modify, and merge a Pull Request after you've created it.

# UNDERSTANDING VIRTUAL FILE SYSTEM

Without having the repository's files on your local computer, you can view file contents and make updates by using the GitHub Repositories extension, which creates a virtual file system in memory. By using a virtual file system, some operations, and extensions that depend on local files are disabled or just partially functional. Capabilities like tasks, debugging, and integrated terminals are not available to connect in the Remote indicator hover, which also offers information about the level of support for the virtual file system.

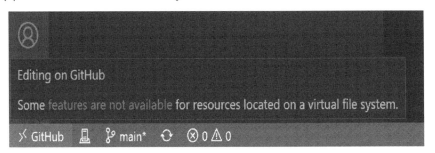

For additional details on using a virtual file system and workspace, refer to the Virtual Workspaces extension author's guide.

You might occasionally want to switch to that environment to work on a repository in a setting that supports a local file system, a full language, and development tools. The GitHub Repositories plugin allows you to easily and quickly:

- If you have the GitHub Codespaces extension, create a codespace on GitHub.
- Clone the repository locally.

- If you have both Docker and the Microsoft Docker extension installed, you can create a Docker container from a cloned repository.

If you want to switch between development environments, use the Continue Working On command. You can access it by clicking on the Remote indication in the Status bar or by using the Command Palette (Ctrl+Shift+P).

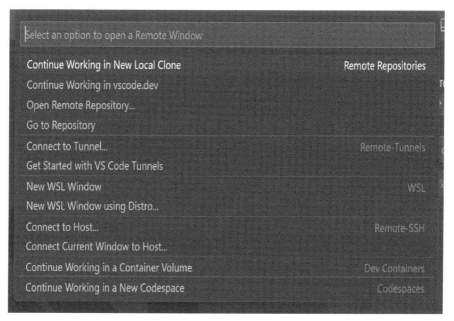

The "Continue Working On..." command in the browser-based editor allows you to choose whether to open the repository locally or in GitHub Codespaces' cloud-hosted environment.

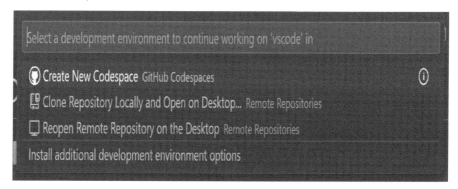

The first time you use Continue Working On with Uncommitted Changes, you will have the option to transfer your adjustments to your preferred development environment using Cloud Changes, which leverages a Visual Studio Code service to store your pending changes.

These updates are withdrawn from our service once they have been applied to your target development environment. If you opt not to commit your uncommitted alterations, you may always change your mind by setting "workbench.cloudChanges.continueOn": "prompt."

# UNDERSTANDING GITHUB COPILOT

To help you code more effectively, Visual Studio Code offers artificial intelligence (AI) tools. They include rapid documentation generation, aid with the creation of code-related artifacts like tests, and suggestions for specific lines of code or entire functions.

Coding is made simpler and faster with GitHub Copilot, an AI-powered code completion tool. You can write new code or learn from generated code by using the GitHub Copilot add-on for Visual Studio Code.

# HOW TO CLONE A REPOSITORY

- • If you haven't previously, you can open a folder from your local computer in the Source Control view or clone the repository.
- •
- The parent directory where the local repository should be stored as well as the URL of the remote repository, such as one on GitHub, will be required information if you select the Clone Repository option.
- You can find the URL for a GitHub repository in the GitHub Code dialog.
- •
- After that, paste that Link into the Git: Clone prompt.
- •

- Moreover, there will be a GitHub Clone option. Once you've logged into Visual Studio Code with your GitHub account, you may browse through repositories by name and select any repo to clone. The cloning of a Git repository can also be started by using the Git: Clone command in the Command Palette (Ctrl+Shift+P). For a detailed walkthrough, see our Clone repos from the Visual Studio Code video.

If you wish to work on a repository without downloading the data to your local machine, take note that you can install the GitHub Repositories extension to view and edit immediately on GitHub. For further details, see the GitHub Repositories extension section.

# UNDERSTANDING STAGING AND COMMITTING

Drag and drop or contextual file operations can be used to stage (git add) or upstaging (git reset). Set up your email and Git username. Be careful that when you commit, Git will default to utilizing information from your local machine if your login and/or email are not specified in your Git settings. The information is contained in the Git commit information.

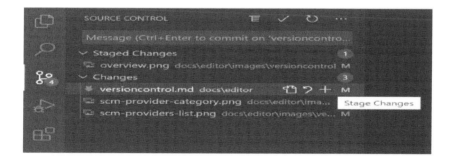

Write a commit message above the changes and press Ctrl+Enter (macOS: +Enter) to save them. If any changes were made, only those that were staged will be committed. Otherwise, you'll be given the option to change your commit settings and asked which changes you want to commit.

For us, this procedure has been effective. The commit will only include the staged changes to overview.png, as can be seen in the preceding snapshot. In subsequent staging and commit procedures, the changes to versioncontrol.md and the two extra.png pictures might be added as a separate commit. More thorough Commit actions are available in the Views and More Actions... menu option at the top of the Source Control view.

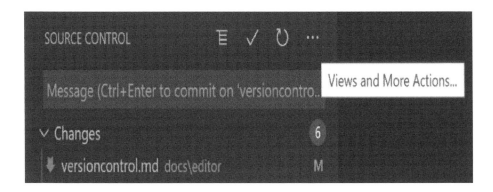

If you unintentionally committed your modification to the wrong branch, use the Git Undo Last Commit command in the Command Palette (Ctrl+Shift+P) to reverse your commit.

# UNDERSTANDING BRANCHES AND TAGS

You may create and checkout branches from within Visual Studio Code by using the commands Git: New Branch and Git: Checkout in the Command Palette (Ctrl+Shift+P).

Running Git: Checkout will provide a dropdown list with all of the branches or tags in the current repository. Also, it will give you the option to build a new branch if you think it would be a better option or to check out an existing branch in detached mode.

With the Git New Branch command, a new branch can be quickly created. To create and switch to a branch, just type its name into Visual Studio Code. By choosing Generate a new branch from..., another option appears, allowing you to decide which commit the new branch should be pointing to.

# UNDERSTANDING MERGE CONFLICTS

Visual Studio Code can identify merge conflicts. The differences are highlighted, and there are inline actions to accept either one of the revisions or both of them. Once the conflicts have been resolved so you can commit the changes, stage the conflicting file.

# UNDERSTANDING REMOTES

If your repository is connected to a remote and your checked-out branch has an upstream link to a branch in that remote, the latter will issue a pull command followed by a push command. Microsoft Studio Code offers you useful methods to push, pull, and sync that branch. These options can be found under the Views and Additional Actions... menu, along with the option to add or remove a remote.

Regular updates for Visual Studio Code can be downloaded from your remotes. By doing this, Visual Studio Code can see how many changes have been done in your local repository as opposed to the remote repository. This function is deactivated by default but can be enabled by using the git.autofetch argument.

You should set up a credential helper if you want to avoid being solicited for credentials each time Visual Studio Code connects to one of your Git remotes. If you don't do this, you might want to consider using the git.autofetch setting to disable automatic fetching to reduce the number of prompts you get.

# UNDERSTANDING GIT STATUS BAR ACTIONS

A Synchronize Changes action is displayed in the Status Bar next to the branch indicator when an upstream branch is set up for the branch that is currently being checked out. After downloading remote updates to your local repository, you can push local commits to the upstream branch by using Synchronize Changes.

If the Git repository has remotes configured but no configured upstream branch, the Publish action is enabled. Now that you've done that, you can publish the current branch to a remote.

# UNDERSTANDING GUTTER INDICATORS

If you open a folder that is a Git repository and begin making changes, Visual Studio Code will add useful comments to the gutter and the overview ruler.

- Line deletions are indicated by red triangles.
- Newly added lines are indicated by a green bar.
- Modified lines are indicated by a blue bar.

```
Program.cs \
 1  using System;
 2
 3 // This is a new line
 4  class Program
 5  {
 6      // this is a comment
 7      public static void Main()
 8      {
 9          var x = 123;
10          Console.WriteLine();
11          Console.WriteLine("hello world!");
12      }
13  }
```

# UNDERSTANDING THE GIT OUTPUT WINDOW

You may easily zoom in to look at the precise Git instructions we are using. This is helpful if anything strange is happening or if you're just curious.

To open the Git output window, go to View > Output and select Log (Git) from the dropdown menu.

# INITIALIZING A REPOSITORY

If your workspace is on your local computer, you can enable Git source control by establishing a Git repository using the Initialize Repository command. If Visual Studio Code is unable to locate a Git repository, you can choose to Initialize the Repository or Publish to GitHub in the Source Control pane.

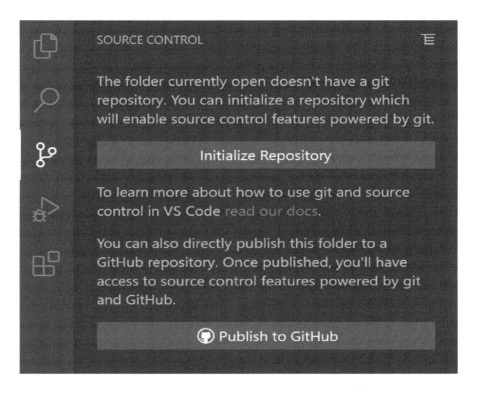

Moreover, you may run the Git Initialize Repository and Publish to GitHub commands using the Command Palette (Ctrl+Shift+P). Initialize Repository will create the pertinent Git repository metadata files, and your workspace files will show up as untracked changes that are prepared for staging. You can decide whether to publish your workspace folder to a private or public repository on GitHub by choosing Publish to GitHub. See our video on publishing repos for more information on publishing to GitHub.

# UNDERSTANDING SCM EXTENSION PROVIDERS

- Git Extension Pack: Well-known Git extensions for Visual Studio Code.
- Integrated Subversion source control is known as SVN.
- Mercurial source control integrated with Hg.
- Perforce for Visual Studio Code: Integration of Perforce with SCM features in Visual Studio Code

In Visual Studio Code, many Source Control providers can be managed at once. For instance, you may easily collaborate on your projects by opening many Git repositories alongside your local Azure DevOps Server workspace. By selecting Views from the overflow menu in the Source Control view (Ctrl+Shift+G), you can enable the Source Control Providers view by selecting the box next to Source Control Repositories. The Source Control Providers tab, which includes the detected providers and repositories, can be narrowed down by choosing a specific provider to display your updates.

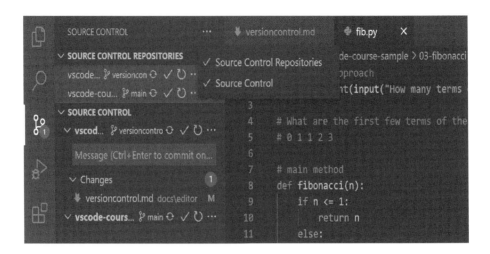

You can search under the SCM Providers extension category in the Extensions view (Ctrl+Shift+X) if you wish to install another SCM provider. As you begin typing "@ca," options for extension categories like debuggers and linters appear. Choose @category:"scm providers" to see the SCM providers that are currently accessible.

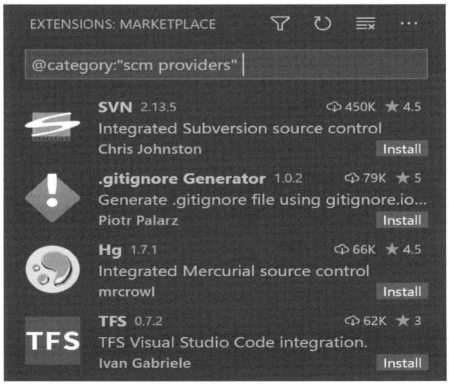

# UNDERSTANDING VISUAL STUDIO CODE AS A GIT EDITOR

When starting Visual Studio Code from the command line, you may have the launch command wait until the new instance of the program has been terminated by using the wait parameter to the command. Git will wait until you close the opened Visual Studio Code instance when Visual Studio Code is configured as your Git external editor. The following are the steps:

- Make sure you can both send and receive help using the command line command code help. If you do not see any help, continue as outlined below.
- To install the "Code" command in the path on Mac OS, select Shell Command from the Command Palette.
- For Windows: Ensure that Add to PATH was selected during installation.
- For Linux: Verify that one of our brand-new .deb or .rpm packages was used to install Code.

```
sers > Admin > Desktop >  index.py
 From the command line, run git config --global core.editor "code --wait".
 Now you can run git config --global -e and use VISUAL STUDIO Code as editor for configuring Git.
```

# CHAPTER FIVE

# UNDERSTANDING DEBUGGING

One of Visual Studio Code's unique characteristics is the superb debugging tools it provides. Using the built-in debugger in Visual Studio Code will speed up the process of editing, compiling, and debugging.

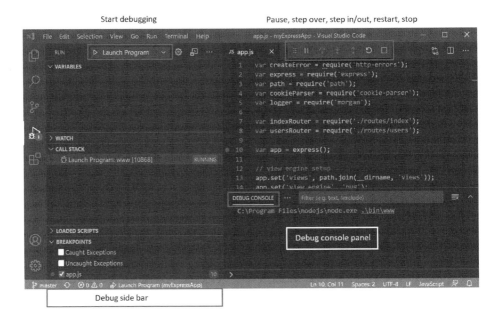

# UNDERSTANDING DEBUGGER EXTENSIONS

JavaScript, TypeScript, and any other language that has been translated to JavaScript may all be debugged with Microsoft Studio Code. Moreover, it offers built-in Node.js runtime debugging support.

To debug additional languages and runtimes, such as PHP, Ruby, Go, C#, Python, C++, PowerShell, and many others, look for Debuggers extensions in the VISUAL STUDIO Code Marketplace or select Install

Additional Debuggers from the top-level Run menu. The list of well-known extensions that facilitate debugging is as follows:

- **Python**: The features include ms-python, IntelliSense (Pylance), Linting, Multi-Threaded Remote Debugging, Jupyter Notebooks, Code Formatting, Refactoring, Unit Testing, and more.
- **C/C++**: ms-Visual Studio code, debugging, code browsing, and C/C++ IntelliSense.
- **Ms-dotnettools in C#:** Visual Studio Code and C# (powered by OmniSharp).
- **Visual Studiocjava**: a compact Java debugger for Visual Studio Code, is a debugger for Java.
- Dynamically questioned extensions are those displayed above. To select which extension is ideal for you, choose a tile from the list above and read the description and reviews.

# HOW TO INITIATE DEBUGGING

The Node.js debugger that comes as standard is the emphasis of the material that follows, however, the majority of the concepts and functionality also apply to other debuggers. To learn about debugging more effectively, it is a good idea to create a test Node.js application first. By following the Node.js guide, you may install Node.js and create a simple "Hello World" JavaScript application (app.js). After setting up a simple application, this page will walk you through Visual Studio Code's debugging options.

# UNDERSTANDING RUN AND DEBUG VIEW

To access the Run and Debug view in Visual Studio Code, select the icon for Run and Debug in the Activity Bar on the side. Another potential keyboard shortcut is Ctrl+Shift+D.

The Run and Debug view shows all running and debugging-related information and has a top bar with debugging commands and configuration options.

If running and debugging is not yet configured, Visual Studio Code shows the Run start view during launch. It has generated json.

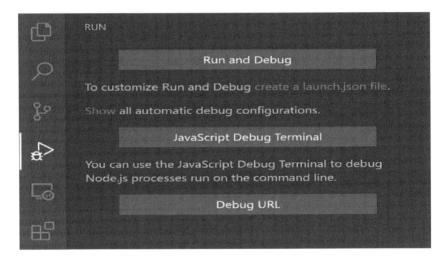

# UNDERSTANDING RUN MENU

The top-level Run menu contains the most used run and debug commands. Check out the image below.

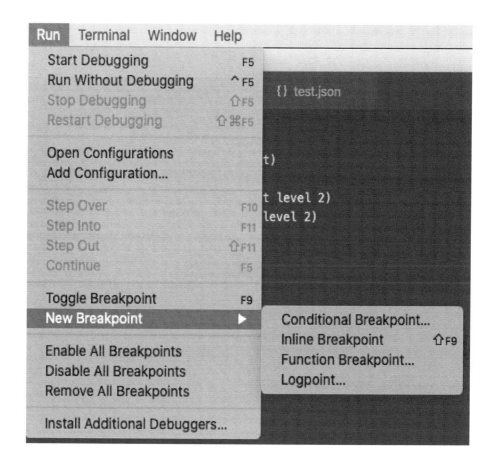

# HOW TO LAUNCH CONFIGURATIONS

To launch or debug a simple app, select Run and Debug from the Debug start pane, or press F5 to have Visual Studio Code try to execute the currently active file.

However, creating a launch configuration file is useful for the majority of debugging situations since it lets you alter and save debugging setup information. Visual Studio Code continues to save configuration data in your workspace (project root folder), user settings, workspace settings, or a launch.json file located in a.VisualStudiocode subfolder. To get going, click the button that says "Build a launch.json file" in the Run start pane.

125

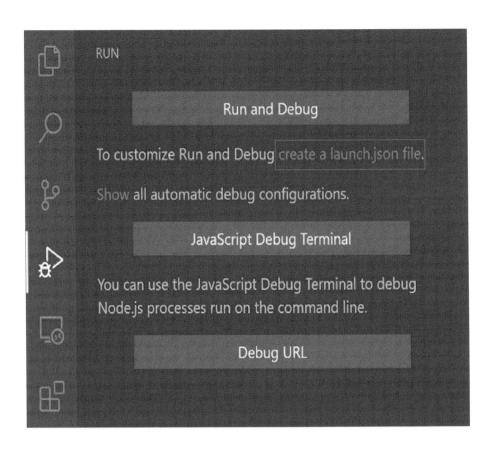

You must specifically choose a debug environment if Visual Studio Code is unable to recognize it automatically.

The launch settings created for Node.js debugging are shown below:

```
{
  "version": "0.2.0",
  "configurations": [
    {
      "type": "node",
      "request": "launch",
      "name": "Launch Program",
      "skipFiles": ["<node_internals>/**"],
      "program": "${workspaceFolder}\\app.js"
    } ] }
```

If you go back to the File Explorer window (Ctrl+Shift+E), you can see that Visual Studio Code added the launch.json file to your workspace and created a.VisualStudiocode folder.

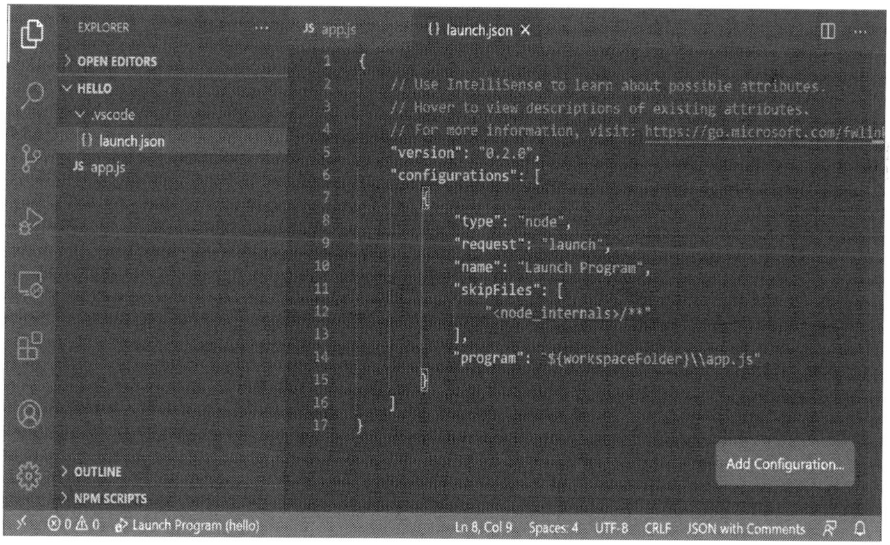

Simple applications can be debugged in Microsoft Studio Code without a folder open, but managing launch configurations and

configuring intricate debugging is not supported. The Visual Studio Code Status Bar turns purple if no folders are open.

It should be noted that various debuggers offer access to various launch configuration attributes. Use IntelliSense recommendations (Ctrl+Space) to find out which characteristics apply to a specific debugger. Hover assistance is accessible for all attributes.

Don't assume that simply because one debugger offers a feature, other debuggers will likewise offer it. Try to fix any green squiggles in your launch setup before beginning a debug session by hovering over them to find out what the problem is.

Check each automatically generated value to ensure it is appropriate for your project and the debugging environment.

# UNDERSTANDING LAUNCH AND ATTACH CONFIGURATIONS

Launch and Attach, which serve two different developer workflows and demographics, are the two main debugging tools in Visual Studio Code. Depending on your process, it can be difficult to select the ideal setup for your project.

If you have used browser development tools before, you might not be accustomed to "launching from your tool" because your browser instance is already open. When accessed, DevTools are merely added to the active browser tab. On the other hand, if you're coming from a server or desktop background, it's rather typical for your editor to launch your process for you and instantly attach your debugger to the recently launched process.

An attach configuration is a recipe for connecting Visual Studio Code's debugger to an app or process that is already running, whereas a launch configuration is a recipe for starting your program in debug mode before Visual Studio Code attaches to it. This comparison demonstrates the distinction between launch and attach.

Normally, you can start a program in debug mode or attach a debugger to an already-running program in debug mode when using the debuggers for Visual Studio Code. Depending on the request (attach or launch), different properties and the launch of Visual Studio Code are required. It should help with JSON validation and recommendations.

## ADDING A FRESH CONFIGURATION

- To include a new configuration to an active launch, use one of the techniques listed below. json:

- Use IntelliSense if your cursor is currently inside the configurations array.
- To enable the snippet IntelliSense, click the Add Configuration button at the start of the array.
- Under Run, select the Add Configuration option.

Visual Studio Code additionally provides compound launch configurations for starting multiple configurations at once; for more details, see this section.

Before starting a debug session, select the configuration under Launch Program using the Configuration dropdown in the Run and Debug pane. Press F5 to start your debug session if your launch settings are prepared. By selecting Debug in the Command Palette (Ctrl+Shift+P), you can alternatively run your setup. Choose the configuration you want to troubleshoot, then press "debug" or click Start Debugging.

As soon as a debugging session starts, the Status Bar changes color (to arrange for default color schemes), and the DEBUG CONSOLE panel appears and shows the debugging output:

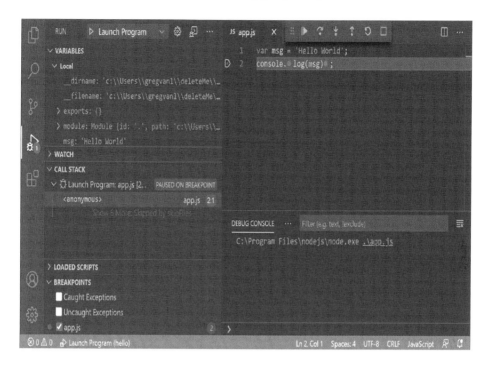

Together with the debug status, the Status Bar also shows the active debug settings. By selecting the debug state, a user can start debugging without first visiting the Run and Debug box and changing the active launch settings.

# UNDERSTANDING DEBUG ACTIONS

Once a debug session has started, the Debug toolbar will appear at the editor's top.

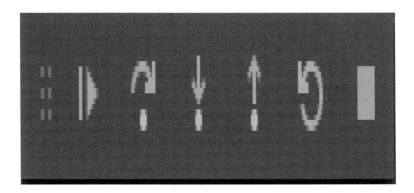

- The following list of deeds and their justifications.
- Continue/Pause (F5) Changing the default script or program execution (up to the next breakpoint).
- Pause: Review the code that is being run at the present line and make line-by-line corrections.
- Step Over F10: Execute the succeeding procedure in a single command, skipping over any of its parts in the process.
- Step Up (F1) To start running the following process line by line, enter it.
- Step for Exit (Shift+F11): When inside a method or subroutine, finish the remaining lines as if it were a single command to exit the current method.
- Restart (Ctrl+Shift+F5): This command causes the program you are now debugging to stop executing and to start again with the same run configuration.
- Stop (Shift+F5): Put an end to the running program.

Use the debug.toolBarLocation property to modify where the debug toolbar displays. You can choose to hide it, dock it to the Run and Debug window, or leave it floating as usual. Slide a floating debug toolbar horizontally and down to the editor area.

# UNDERSTANDING RUN MODE

In addition to debugging programs, Visual Studio Code supports running them. The Debug: Run Start Without Debugging action, which makes use of the chosen launch configuration, is started by pressing the keys Ctrl and F5. Numerous launch configuration attributes are supported in "Run" mode. Microsoft Studio Code keeps a debug session open while the program is running; selecting the Stop button closes the application.

Although it is always available, not all debugger extensions support the Run operation. In this case, "Run" will be similar to "Debug."

# UNDERSTANDING BREAKPOINTS

Breakpoints can be toggled by clicking on the editor margin or by hitting F9 on the current line. More exact breakpoint control (enable/disable/reapply) is available in the BREAKPOINTS section of the Run and Debug view.

- In the editor margin, breakpoints are often represented by red-filled circles.
- Disabled breakpoints have a filled gray circle.
- When a debugging session starts, breakpoints that the debugger cannot register change into a gray hollow circle. The same thing can happen if the code is modified while a debug session without live-edit features is running.

Any failures or exceptions that the debugger allows breaking on will also be shown in the BREAKPOINTS pane.

Reapply All Breakpoints is a command that resets all breakpoints to their original locations. This is helpful if your debugging environment is "lazy" and "misplaces" breakpoints in unrun source code.

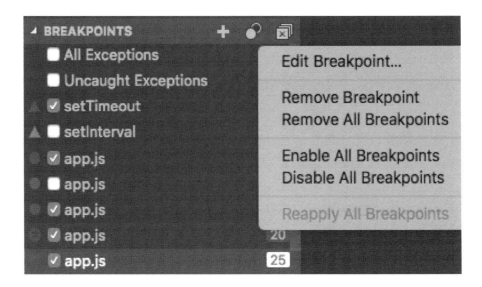

Breakpoints can optionally be shown in the editor's overview ruler by using the debug setting.showBreakpointsInOverviewRuler:

```
378
379     return config;
380 }
381
382 v function loadJSON(folder: vscode.WorkspaceFolder | undefined, file: string): any {
383 v     if (folder) {
384 v         try {
385             const path = join(folder.uri.fsPath, file);
386             const content = fs.readFileSync(path, 'utf8');
387             return JSON.parse(content);
388 v         } catch (error) {
389             // silently ignore
390         }
391     }
```

# UNDERSTANDING LOGPOINTS

An alternative to "breaking" into the debugger, a logpoint reports a message to the console. For debugging production servers that cannot be stopped or paused, logpoints are especially helpful. A Logpoint is represented by a symbol in the form of a "diamond". Log messages are still plain text even though they may contain expressions to be evaluated inside curly brackets (").

Like traditional breakpoints, logpoints can be enabled or disabled, and they can also be controlled by a condition and/or hit count. Logpoints are supported by the VISUAL STUDIO Code Node.js debugger, but they can also be used by other debug extensions. The Python and Java extensions, respectively, both support logpoints.

# UNDERSTANDING DATA INSPECTION

Hovering over a variable's source in the editor or the VARIABLES section of the Run and Debug view will reveal its source for inspection. The selected stack frame affects the values of variables and the evaluation of expressions in the CALL STACK section.

Variable values can be modified using the Change Value action that can be found in the variable's context menu. Moreover, you can duplicate an expression using the Copy as Expression action or copy the variable's value by using the Copy Value action.

Variables and expressions can also be evaluated and watched in the Run and Debug view's WATCH section.

Typing can be used to filter the variable names and values when the VARIABLES section is under focus.

# UNDERSTANDING LAUNCH.JSON ATTRIBUTES

To support multiple debuggers and debugging circumstances, a large number of launch.json attributes are accessible. As previously mentioned, after entering a value for the type attribute, you can browse the list of available characteristics using IntelliSense (Ctrl+Space).

- The following requirements must be met by every launch configuration:

- **type**: This launch configuration's type determines the kind of debugger to use. Each debug extension that is installed introduces a type: While Node can access the internal Node debugger, PHP and Go can access the PHP and Go extensions.
- **request**: This launch configuration's specific request type. Launch and attach are supported at the moment.
- **name**: The name that will be displayed in the menu for the Debug launch option and is readable.

For all launch configurations, the following attributes are available and optional:

- **Presentation**: You can use the order, group, and hidden attributes in the presentation object to sort, group, and hide configurations and compounds in the Debug configuration dropdown and the Debug quick pick.
- **preLaunchTask**: To launch a task before the start of a debug session, set this attribute to the label of a task given in tasks.json (in the workspace's.VisualStudiocode folder). By setting this to $defaultBuildTask, you can use your default build task instead.
- **postDebugTask**: To run a task at the very end of a debug session, set this attribute to the name of the task specified in tasks.json (in the workspace's.VisualStudio code folder).
- **internalConsoleOptions:** This attribute controls the visibility of the Debug Console window while debugging is taking place.
- **debugServer**: solely available to authors of debug extensions, this feature allows you to connect to a specific port without first launching the debug adapter.
- **serverReadyAction**: If a certain message is an output to the debug console or integrated terminal when a program is being debugged, you can use the serverReadyAction command to open a URL in a web browser. Check out the section below labeled "Open a URI automatically when debugging a server program" for additional details.

A lot of debuggers provide the following characteristics:

- **program**: When the debugger is launched, this executable file will be run.
- **args**: The debugging parameters for the application.
- Env: Environment variables (env) allow for the "undefinition" of a variable by using the value null.
- • envFile: The location of the environment variables' .env file.
- **cwd**: Represent the location of the current working directory, where further files and dependencies can be found.
- **port**: When connecting to an active process, use a port.
- **stopOnEntry**: Terminate the program as soon as it starts.
- **console**: Choose among an internal console, a terminal that is incorporated, or an external terminal.

# UNDERSTANDING VARIABLE SUBSTITUTION

Frequently used paths and other values are available in Visual Studio Code as variables, and launch.json supports variable substitution inside strings. This suggests that it is not necessary to use absolute paths in debug settings. For instance, ${workspaceFolder} represents the root-path of a work environment (workspace) folder, ${file} represents the file open in the active editor, and ${env:Name} the environment variable 'Name'. In the Variables Guide or by utilizing IntelliSense inside the string attributes of launch.json, a comprehensive list of pre-set variables is accessible.

```
{
  "type": "node",
  "request": "launch",
  "name": "Launch Program",
  "program": "${workspaceFolder}/app.js",
  "cwd": "${workspaceFolder}",
  "args": ["${env:USERNAME}"]
}
```

# UNDERSTANDING PLATFORM-SPECIFIC PROPERTIES

You can supply data (such as program arguments) that depend on the operating system that the debugger is running on using Launch.json. Create a platform-specific literal and define the required properties in it in the launch.json file. The following is an illustration of an alternative approach to delivering "args" to a program on Windows:

```json
{
  "version": "0.2.0",
  "configurations": [
    {
      "type": "node",
      "request": "launch",
      "name": "Launch Program",
      "program": "${workspaceFolder}/node_modules/gulp/bin/gulpfile.js",
      "args": ["myFolder/path/app.js"],
      "windows": {
        "args": ["myFolder\\path\\app.js"]
      }
    }]
}
```

The operating attributes "windows" for Windows, "linux" for Linux, and "osx" for macOS are all allowed. Properties declared under an operating system-specific scope are given priority over those defined globally.

Because the type indirectly determines the platform in remote debugging situations, causing a circular dependency, the type property cannot be placed within a platform-specific section. Except for macOS, debugging the program in the example below always terminates when it starts:

```json
{
  "version": "0.2.0",
  "configurations": [
    {
      "type": "node",
      "request": "launch",
      "name": "Launch Program",
      "program": "${workspaceFolder}/node_modules/gulp/bin/gulpfile.js",
      "stopOnEntry": true,
      "osx": {
        "stopOnEntry": false
      }
    }
  ]
}
```

# UNDERSTANDING GLOBAL LAUNCH CONFIGURATION

The "launch" object can be added in Visual Studio Code's User settings. Then, all of your workspaces will use this "launch" setting. For instance:

```json
"launch": {
  "version": "0.2.0",
  "configurations": [{
    "type": "node",
    "request": "launch",
    "name": "Launch Program",
    "program": "${file}"
  }]
}
```

# UNDERSTANDING CONDITIONAL BREAKPOINTS

A powerful debugging tool in Visual Studio Code is the capability to create conditions based on expressions, hit counts, or a combination of the two.

- **Expression condition**: The breakpoint will be reached if the expression evaluates to true.
- **Hit count**: This parameter determines how many times a breakpoint must be reached before execution is "broken." The actual syntax of the phrase and respect for a "hit count" varies amongst debugger extensions.

You can define a condition and/or hit count using the Edit Condition action when adding a source breakpoint using the Add Conditional Breakpoint action or changing an existing one. A selectable text box with an inline text field where you can type words appears in both scenarios.

Support for condition and hit count modification is also included for function and exception breakpoints. You can begin the condition adjustment procedure from the context menu or the new inline Edit Condition action. Example of BREAKPOINTS view condition modification.

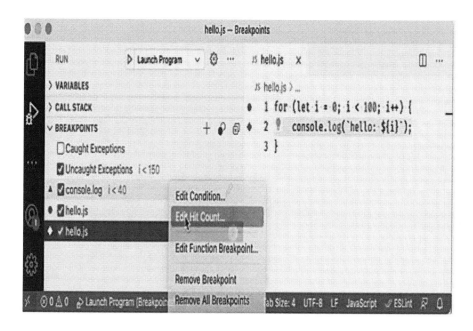

If a debugger doesn't support conditional breakpoints, the Add Conditional Breakpoint and Change Condition actions won't be available.

# UNDERSTANDING INLINE BREAKPOINTS

Only when the execution reaches the corresponding column do inline breakpoints become active. When troubleshooting code that has been minified and has multiple statements on a single line, this is quite helpful.

During a debug session, you can establish an inline breakpoint by pressing Shift+F9 or using the context menu. Inline breakpoints are seen in the editor. Inline breakpoints can also have conditions. You can edit many breakpoints on a single line using the context menu located in the editor's left margin.

# UNDERSTANDING FUNCTION BREAKPOINTS

Rather than placing them directly in the source code, a debugger can support setting breakpoints by providing the name of a function. This is useful if the name of a function is known but the source is not available.

One can create a function breakpoint by clicking the Add button in the BREAKPOINTS section header and entering the function name. Function breakpoints are shown in the BREAKPOINTS section as red triangles.

# UNDERSTANDING DATA BREAKPOINTS

If a debugger supports them, data breakpoints can be set via the context menu in the VARIABLES view. The Break on Value Change/Read/Access commands add a data breakpoint that is reached when the value of the underlying variable changes is read or accessed. Data breakpoints are shown as red hexagons in the BREAKPOINTS section.

# UNDERSTANDING DEBUG CONSOLE REPL

Expressions can be evaluated using the Debug Console's Read-Eval-Print Loop (REPL) feature. To access the Debug Console, use the View: Debug Console command (Ctrl+Shift+Y) or the Debug Console action at the top of the Debug window. Expressions are evaluated after you press Enter, and the Debug Console REPL offers suggestions as you type. When inputting multiple lines, use Shift+Enter to jump between them and Enter to send them all for review. Debug Console input takes advantage of the active editor's mode, making it compatible with other linguistic features like syntax highlighting, indentation, and auto-closing quotes.

```
DEBUG CONSOLE
node --debug-brk=43743 --nolazy fib.js
Debugger listening on port 43743
89

enabled
false
7 + 8
15
range
▲ Object ⓘ
  ▶ child: Object
    endLineNumber: 8
    startColumn: 123
    startLineNumber: 7
    te: "11"
    te6: "11"
    text: "lineContext.getTokenEndIndex(tokenIndex) + 1"
  fib(15)
  987

> |
```

Keep in mind that a debug session must be open to using the Debug Console REPL.

# INPUT/OUTPUT IS REDIRECTED TO/FROM THE DEBUG TARGET

There isn't a built-in solution for all debuggers in Visual Studio Code because input/output redirection depends on the debugger or runtime. Here are two strategies you might want to take into account:

- Manually launch the debugging program ("debug target") at a command prompt or terminal and reroute input and output as necessary. Make sure the correct command line arguments are supplied to the debug target to allow a debugger to attach to it. It is necessary to develop and run a "attach" debug configuration that connects to the debug target.

145

- If the debugger extension you're using can run the debug target in VISUAL STUDIO Code's Integrated Terminal, you might try giving the shell redirect syntax (for example, "" or ">") as parameters or an external terminal.

An instance of the launch.json configuration is provided below:

```
{
    "name": "launch program that reads a file from stdin",
    "type": "node",
    "request": "launch",
    "program": "program.js",
    "console": "integratedTerminal",
    "args": ["<", "in.txt"]
}
```

This approach requires the "" syntax to be transmitted via the debugger extension and to enter the Integrated Terminal intact.

# UNDERSTANDING MULTI-TARGET DEBUGGING

Debugging multiple targets is possible in Visual Studio Code for complex scenarios involving numerous processes (such as a client and a server).

It is simple to use multi-target debugging; after starting one debug session, you can immediately begin another. Once a second session has begun, the Visual Studio Code user interface switches to multi-target mode: Individual sessions are now shown as top-level entries in the CALL STACK view.

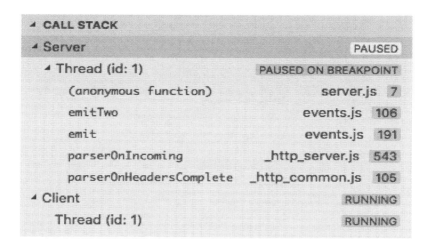

The debug toolbar displays the currently active session, and a dropdown menu provides access to all additional sessions.

The current session is affected by all debug actions, including those displayed in the debug toolbar. The active session can be changed by either selecting a different element in the CALL STACK view or by using the dropdown menu in the debug toolbar.

# UNDERSTANDING COMPOUND LAUNCH CONFIGURATIONS

Another way to initiate several debug sessions is by using a compound launch configuration. A compound launch configuration lists the names of two or more launch configurations that should be launched simultaneously. Before the beginning of each distinct debug session, a preLaunchTask that is optional can be defined. Depending on the value of the boolean flag stopAll, if one session is manually ended, all of the compound sessions will also end.

```json
{
    "version": "0.2.0",
    "configurations": [
        {
            "type": "node",
            "request": "launch",
            "name": "Server",
            "program": "${workspaceFolder}/server.js"
        },
        {
            "type": "node",
            "request": "launch",
            "name": "Client",
            "program": "${workspaceFolder}/client.js"
        }
    ],
    "compounds": [
        {
            "name": "Server/Client",
            "configurations": ["Server", "Client"],
            "preLaunchTask": "${defaultBuildTask}",
            "stopAll": true
        } ] }
```

Compound launch settings are displayed in the launch configuration dropdown menu.

# UNDERSTANDING REMOTE DEBUGGING

The debug extension you are using has a capability called remote debugging; Visual Studio Code itself does not have this feature. Please go to the extension's website in the Marketplace for assistance and information.

There is, however, one exception: Visual Studio Code's integrated Node.js debugger supports remote debugging. Read the online documentation for Node.js Debugging to learn how to configure this.

# WHEN DEBUGGING A SERVER PROGRAM, HOW TO AUTOMATICALLY OPEN A URI

When creating web software, opening a specific URL in a web browser is frequently necessary to gain access to the server code in the debugger. The "serverReadyAction" built-in function in Visual Studio Code makes it possible to automate this operation. An example of a simple Node.js Express application is shown below.

```javascript
var express = require('express');
var app = express();
app.get('/', function(req, res) {
  res.send('Hello World!');
});
app.listen(3000, function() {
  console.log('Example app listening on port 3000!');
});
```

This software initially installs the "Hello World" handler for the "/" URL before starting to listen on port 3000 for HTTP connections. After the port was specified in the Debug Console, the developer would typically now enter http://localhost:3000 into their browser application.

The serverReadyAction feature allows each launch configuration to add the structural property serverReadyAction and select an "action" to be performed:

```
{
  "type": "node",
  "request": "launch",
  "name": "Launch Program",
  "program": "${workspaceFolder}/app.js",
  "serverReadyAction": {
    "pattern": "listening on port ([0-9]+)",
    "uriFormat": "http://localhost:%s",
    "action": "openExternally"
  }
}
```

The pattern attribute in this example describes the regular expression used to match the output string of the program that advertises the port. The port number pattern is put in parenthesis so that it can be used as a regular expression capture group. It is possible to acquire the complete URI even if in this example we are only extracting the port number.

The uriFormat attribute provides information about the format of the URI generated from the port number. The matching pattern's first capture group takes the place of the first%. After that, the produced URI is opened externally ("outside of Visual Studio Code") using the default program that was configured for the URI's scheme.

# UNDERSTANDING TRIGGER DEBUGGING VIA MICROSOFT EDGE OR CHROME

As an alternative, you may utilize the actions debugWithEdge or debugWithChrome. In this mode, a webRoot property that is sent to the debug session for Chrome or Edge can be included. To keep things a little bit simpler, most properties are optional, and we default to the following values:

- **pattern**: "listening on.* (https?://\\S+|[0-9]+)". This resembles the notifications "listening on port 3000" or "Currently listening on https://localhost:5001" that are frequently seen.
- **uriFormat**: http://localhost:%s.
- **webRoot**: "${workspaceFolder}".

# UNDERSTANDING HOW TO ACTIVATE AN ARBITRAL LAUNCH CONFIGURATION

In other cases, you might need to change to a different debugger entirely or add more options to the browser debug session. To do this, set startDebugging as the value of the action property's name property, which should be set to the name of the launch configuration when the pattern is matched. The recognized launch configuration and the serverReadyAction need to be in the same file or folder.

Here is an example of the serverReadyAction functionality:

# CHAPTER SIX

# EXTERNAL TOOLS AND TASK AUTOMATION

To automate tasks like developing, testing, packaging, and deploying software systems, there are many tools at our disposal. A few examples are the TypeScript Compiler, linters such as ESLint and TSLint, and build tools such as Make, Ant, Gulp, Jake, Rake, and MSBuild.

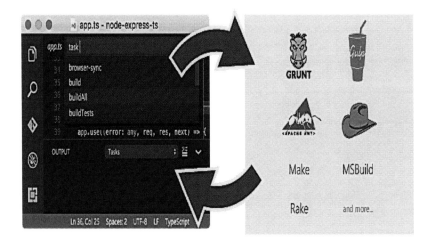

These programs, which are often run from the command line, automate processes both inside and outside of the internal software development cycle (edit, compile, test, and debug). Given the importance of tools in the development life cycle, it is advantageous to be able to use Microsoft Studio Code to execute them and assess their results. Because tasks in Visual Studio Code may be configured to run scripts and processes, many of the current tools can be used there without the need to enter a command line or write new code. The workspace contains the tasks.json file. To set up tasks specific to a workspace or folder, use the Visual Studio code folder.

Extensions can contribute tasks using a Task Provider, and these tasks may contain workspace-specific parameters defined in the tasks.json file. Remember that using a workspace folder is the only time when task support is provided. It is not accessible when editing a single file.

## TypeScript Hello World

Let's start by translating a simple TypeScript "Hello World" program into JavaScript. Create a tsconfig.json file, a blank folder called "mytask," and start Visual Studio Code from that location.

```
mkdir mytask
cd mytask
tsc --init
code .
Now create a HelloWorld.ts file with the following content
function sayHello(name: string): void {
  console.log(`Hello ${name}!`);
}
sayHello('Dave');
```

The following picker appears when you press Ctrl+Shift+B or select Run Build Task from the global Terminal menu:

The TypeScript compiler is started in the first line, which transforms the TypeScript file into a JavaScript file. When the compiler is complete, a HelloWorld.js file should exist. The second entry launches the TypeScript compiler in watch mode. The HelloWorld.js file is created each time the HelloWorld.ts file is saved.

You can designate the TypeScript build or watch task as the default build job to guarantee that it is carried out instantly when Run Build Task (Ctrl+Shift+B) is activated. To do this, select Establish Default Build Task from the global Terminal menu. With this picker, the available construction tasks are shown. If you select tsc: build or tsc:

153

watch, Visual Studio Code will produce the tasks.json file. The following command makes the tsc the default build job: build task:

```json
{
    // See https://go.microsoft.com/fwlink/?LinkId=733558
    // for the documentation about the tasks.json format
    "version": "2.0.0",
    "tasks": [
        {
            "type": "typescript",
            "tsconfig": "tsconfig.json",
            "problemMatcher": ["$tsc"],
            "group": {
                "kind": "build",
                "isDefault": true
            }
        }]
}
```

The responsibilities described above. The json sample doesn't offer a brand-new task. It designates the TypeScript extension of Visual Studio Code's tsc: build tasks as the default build task. The TypeScript compiler can now be invoked by pressing Ctrl+Shift+B.

# UNDERSTANDING TASK AUTO-DETECTION

Now, Visual Studio Code detects Gulp, Grunt, Jake, and npm tasks automatically. We are working with the creators of the corresponding extensions to enable support for Maven and the C# dotnet command as well. If you construct a JavaScript application using Node.js as the runtime, you normally have a package.json file outlining your dependencies and the scripts to execute. If you duplicated the eslint-starter example, running Run Tasks from the global menu displays the list below.

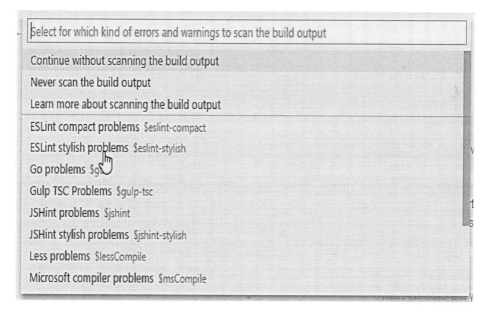

If you haven't already, use the npm install command to install the necessary npm modules. Now open the server.js file, and use a semicolon to end each statement. The ESLint starter runs the tasks again after assuming statements without a semicolon. this time, select the npm: lint task. Choose ESLint stylish as the problem matcher to use when prompted. During task execution, one mistake is committed and is shown in the problem view.

A tasks.json file was also produced by Visual Studio Code and contained the following information:

```
{
  // See https://go.microsoft.com/fwlink/?LinkId=733558
  // for the documentation about the tasks.json format
  "version": "2.0.0",
  "tasks": [
    {
      "type": "npm",
      "script": "lint",
      "problemMatcher": ["$eslint-stylish"]
    }] }
```

This instructs Visual Studio Code to inspect the output of the npm lint script for bugs using the ESLint style format.

Gulp, Grunt, and Jake all utilize the same task auto-detection system. The example below displays the jobs discovered for the Visual Studiocode-node-debug extension.

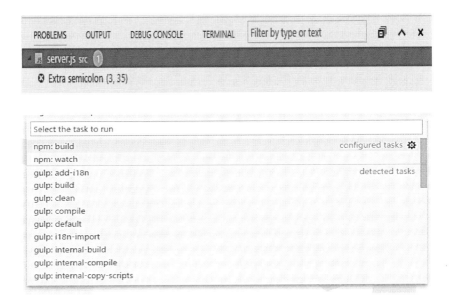

When using Quick Open (Ctrl+P), type "task," a space, then the command name to run your task. Namely, "task lint."

The following options can be used to prevent task auto-detection:

```
{

  "typescript.tsc.autoDetect": "off",

  "grunt.autoDetect": "off",

  "jake.autoDetect": "off",

  "gulp.autoDetect": "off",

  "npm.autoDetect": "off"

}
```

# UNDERSTANDING CUSTOM TASKS

Not every job or script in your workspace can be recognized automatically. Sometimes, it's necessary to specify your special responsibilities. Assume you have a script that will execute your tests to ensure an environment is configured appropriately. The script is kept in a script folder inside your workspace and has the names test.sh for Linux and macOS and test.cmd for Windows. When launching Configure Tasks from the global Terminal menu, select the Create tasks.json file from the template entry option. This displays the picker you see below:

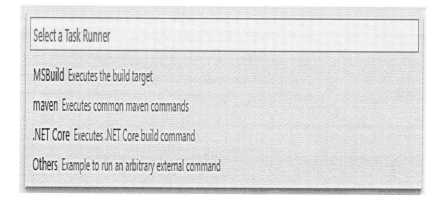

If you don't see the list of task runner templates, a tasks.json file can already be there and open in the editor in your folder. Close the file and then choose to either rename it or delete it for this example.

As we work to enhance auto-detection support, this list will keep becoming shorter. Since we want to develop a special activity, select Others from the list. When the tasks.json file is accessed, a task skeleton is shown. Insert the following code in its place.

```json
{
    // See https://go.microsoft.com/fwlink/?LinkId=733558
    // for the documentation about the tasks.json format
    "version": "2.0.0",
    "tasks": [
        {
            "label": "Run tests",
            "type": "shell",
            "command": "./scripts/test.sh",
            "windows": {
                "command": ".\\scripts\\test.cmd"
            },
            "group": "test",
            "presentation": {
                "reveal": "always",
                "panel": "new"
            }
        }
    ]
}
```

The following semantic describes the qualities of the task.

- **label**: The user interface's label for the task.
- **Type**: The type of task can either be processed for a bespoke task or used as a shell task. If a shell is provided, such as bash, cmd, or PowerShell, the command is executed as a shell command. If the process is provided, the command is interpreted as an executable process.
- **command**: The directive to be carried out.

158

- **windows**: Any Windows-specific functionality. The command will be used in place of the default properties when it is used with the Windows operating system.
- **group**: Shows which group the work belongs to. In the example, it belongs to the test group. You can execute tasks that are a part of the test group by selecting Run Test Task from the Command Palette.
- **presentation**: Describes how the job output will be handled by the user interface. In this example, each time a job is done, a new terminal is created and the integrated terminal showing the output is constantly visible.
- **options**: Modify the default values for the shell, environment variables, or current working directory default shell. Each assignment, the platform, the entire globe, or both may have parameters set. Environment variables defined here can only be referred to from within your task script or process; they will not be resolved if they are included in your command, args, or other task characteristics.
- **runOptions**: Explain how and when a task is to be completed.

Using IntelliSense in your tasks, you can view all task properties and values. the json file Use Trigger Suggest (Ctrl+Space) to bring up ideas, and then use the Read More. I fly out or hover to read the descriptions.

```
{} tasks.json  ×

.vscode > tasks.json > tasks > 0
    1    {
    2        "version": "2.0.0",
    3        "tasks": [
    4            {
    5                "label": "echo",
    6                "type": "shell",
    7                "command": "echo Hello",
    8                |
    9            }          args
   10        ]          dependsOn
   11    }              dependsOrder
                        group
                        isBackground              ①
                        linux
                        options
                        osx
                        presentation
                        problemMatcher
                        promptOnClose
                        runOptions
```

The tasks can also be examined using the schema for json. Shell commands need to be treated differently when commands or parameters contain spaces or other special characters like $. The following actions are supported by the task system by default:

The task system transmits a single command if given, directly to the underlying shell. If quotes or escape characters are necessary for the command to function properly, they must be included in the command. For instance, the ls 'folder with spaces' bash command can be used to list the directory of a folder with spaces in its name.

```
{
    "label": "dir",
    "type": "shell",
    "command": "dir 'folder with spaces'"
}
```

When a command and parameters are given, the task system will use single quotes if the command or arguments contain spaces. For cmd.exe, double quotation marks are used. A shell command will be executed by PowerShell as dir "folder with spaces."

160

```
{
    "label": "dir",
    "type": "shell",
    "command": "dir",
    "args": ["folder with spaces"]
}
```

If you want to customize how it is quoted, the parameter can be a literal defining the value and a quotation style. In the sentence with spaces below, escaping is used in place of quoting.

```
{
    "label": "dir",
    "type": "shell",
    "command": "dir",
    "args": [
        {
            "value": "folder with spaces",
            "quoting": "escape"     }] }
```

Besides escape, the following values are supported:

- **strong**: Utilizes the shell's strong quoting capability to turn off all string assessments. In the PowerShell, Linux, and macOS shells, single quotes are utilized ('). " is the syntax for cmd.exe.
- **weak**: use the weak quoting feature of the shell, which still evaluates the internal expression of the string (for example, environment variables). In Linux, Mac OS, and PowerShell shells, double quotes are used " ("). Because Visual Studio Code uses ", cmd.exe does not allow weak quoting.

If the command has any spaces, Visual Studio Code will by default strongly quote it as well. The command quotation can be changed by the user using the same literal method as for parameters.

You can configure your process using a variety of task settings. A list of valid properties can be viewed using IntelliSense and Ctrl+Space.

```
"windows": {
    "command": ".\\scripts\\test.cmd"
},
"group": "test",
```

```
🔧 args                                              ⓘ
🔧 dependsOn
🔧 identifier
🔧 isBackground
🔧 linux
🔧 options
🔧 osx
🔧 problemMatcher
🔧 promptOnClose
🔧 suppressTaskName
```

Now, in addition to the global menu bar, task commands can also be accessed from the Command Palette (Ctrl+Shift+P). When you filter on "task," all of the various commands connected to tasks are accessible.

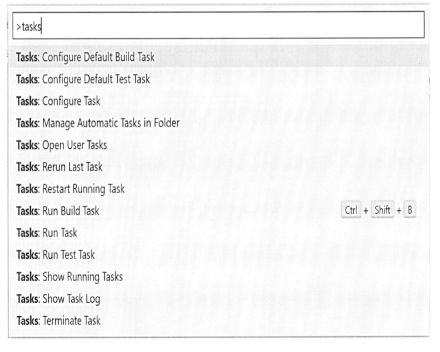

# UNDERSTANDING COMPOUND TASKS

The dependsOn property allows you to combine simpler operations to produce more complicated ones. You can make a task that opens client and server folders in separate terminal windows, for example, if your workspace has client and server directories with build scripts in each. When more than one job is listed in the dependsOn field, they are all executed concurrently by default. These are the assignments. The json file is displayed.

```json
{
  "version": "2.0.0",
  "tasks": [
    {
      "label": "Client Build",
      "command": "gulp",
      "args": ["build"],
      "options": {
        "cwd": "${workspaceFolder}/client"
      } },
    {
      "label": "Server Build",
      "command": "gulp",
      "args": ["build"],
      "options": {
        "cwd": "${workspaceFolder}/server"
      }},
    {
      "label": "Build",
      "dependsOn": ["Client Build", "Server Build"]
    } ] }
```

If you specify "dependsOrder": "sequence," your task dependents are executed in the order they are listed in dependsOn. The issue matcher used in dependsOn with "dependsOrder": "sequence" must keep track of the completion of any background or watch jobs. The following tasks are Task One, Task Two, Task Three, and Task Four.

```
{
    "label": "One",
    "type": "shell",
    "command": "echo Hello ",
    "dependsOrder": "sequence",
    "dependsOn": ["Two", "Three"]
}
```

# UNDERSTANDING USER-LEVEL TASKS

You can create user-level tasks that are not restricted to a certain workspace or folder by using the Tasks Open User Tasks command. Only shell and process tasks can be used in this scenario since other task types require workspace information.

# UNDERSTANDING OUTPUT BEHAVIOR

The behavior of the Integrated Terminal panel can occasionally be changed when executing tasks. Making the most of the editor's space, for instance, might entail only checking the task output when something seems off. The behavior of the terminal can be managed using a task's presentation property. It features the following things:

- **reveal**: Decides whether to bring the Integrated Terminal panel to the front. Valid values include
- **always**: The panel is brought to the front at all times. This is the standard.
- **never**: The View > Terminal command (Ctrl+') must be used to specifically display the terminal panel to the front.

- **silent:** Only when the output is not checked for errors and warnings is the terminal panel brought to the front.
- **revealProblems:** Determines whether or not the Issues panel is displayed when this job is run. is more important than option revelation. Never is the default.
- **always:** When this job is run, the Issues panel is always displayed.
- When an issue is discovered, the problem only displays the Problems panel.
- **never:** When this job is run, the Issues panel is never displayed.
- **focus:** Determines whether or not the terminal is accepting input focus. False is the default.
- **echo:** Determines whether the terminal will echo the command that was just executed. The default is yes.
- **terminal:** The message "Terminal will be reused by tasks, hit any key to close it" is controlled by the showReuseMessage setting.
- **panel:** This setting determines whether the terminal instance is used for multiple task executions. Possible values include:
- **shared:** The terminal is used for many tasks, and their output is added to it.
- **devoted:** The terminal is focused on a single task. The terminal is utilized once again if that task is repeated. Yet, a different task's output is displayed in a different terminal.
- **new:** Each time the task is executed, a brand-new, empty terminal is used.
- **clear:** Determines whether the terminal is cleared before executing this job. False is the default.
- **close:** Determines whether the task's running terminal will be shut down after it is finished.
- **terminal group:** Uses split windows to determine whether the task is performed in a specific terminal group. Tasks that are

part of the same group and are identified by a string value will be presented in split terminals rather than a new terminal panel.

You can alter how the terminal panel responds to automatically recognized jobs. The presentation property, for instance, could be added to the npm: To change the output behavior in the ESLint example from above, use the lint command:

```
{
  // See https://go.microsoft.com/fwlink/?LinkId=733558
  // for the documentation about the tasks.json format
  "version": "2.0.0",
  "tasks": [
    {
      "type": "npm",
      "script": "lint",
      "problemMatcher": ["$eslint-stylish"],
      "presentation": {
        "reveal": "never"
      } }] }
```

Moreover, you can mix configurations for recognized jobs with unique tasks. An example of a tasks.json that adds a unique Run Test job and sets up the npm is the following: run lint task:

```json
{
  // See https://go.microsoft.com/fwlink/?LinkId=733558
  // for the documentation about the tasks.json format
  "version": "2.0.0",
  "tasks": [
    {
      "type": "npm",
      "script": "lint",
      "problemMatcher": ["$eslint-stylish"],
      "presentation": {
        "reveal": "never"
      } },
    {
      "label": "Run tests",
      "type": "shell",
      "command": "./scripts/test.sh",
      "windows": {
        "command": ".\\scripts\\test.cmd"
      },
      "group": "test",
      "presentation": {
        "reveal": "always",
        "panel": "new"
      }}] }
```

# UNDERSTANDING RUN BEHAVIOR

A task's run operations can be specified using the runOptions property:

- reevaluateOnRerun: When the Rerun Last Task command is used, this setting controls how variables are evaluated while a task is being executed. Variables will be reevaluated when a job is restarted because the default value is true. If false is set, the resolved variable values from the task's previous execution will be utilized.
- runOn: Defines the time a job is executed.

- **by default**: Only when the Run Task command is used will the task be carried out.
- **folderOpen**: The task will be carried out when the included folder is opened. When you use folderOpen to open a folder that includes a task for the first time, you will be requested to confirm your desire to allow tasks to execute automatically in that folder. By utilizing the Manage Automatic Tasks command later on, you can decide whether to Allow Automatic Tasks or Disallow Automatic Tasks.

# CONFIGURATION OF AUTO-DETECTED TASKS

As was already said, you can change tasks that are automatically recognized by using the tasks.json file. Typically, you would use this to change the presentation settings or to attach an issue matcher to verify the task's output for errors and warnings. You can change a task directly from the Run Task list by selecting the gear icon to the right of a job and adding the necessary task refers to the tasks.json file. To lint JavaScript scripts with ESLint, you will need the Gulp file below, which can be found at https://github.com/adametry/gulp-eslint:

```
const gulp = require('gulp');
const eslint = require('gulp-eslint');
gulp.task('lint', () => {
  // ESLint ignores files with "node_modules" paths.
  // So, it's best to have gulp ignore the directory as well.
  // Also, Be sure to return the stream from the task;
  // Otherwise, the task may end before the stream has finished.
  return (
    gulp
      .src(['**/*.js', '!node_modules/**'])
      // eslint() attaches the lint output to the "eslint" property
      // of the file object so it can be used by other modules.
      .pipe(eslint())
      // eslint.format() outputs the lint results to the console.
      // Alternatively use eslint.formatEach() (see Docs).
      .pipe(eslint.format())
      // To have the process exit with an error code (1) on
      // lint error, return the stream and pipe to failAfterError last.
      .pipe(eslint.failAfterError())
  );
});
gulp.task('default', ['lint'], function() {
  // This will only run if the lint task is successful...
});
```

Start Run Task from the global Terminal menu to view the following picker. Make use of the gear symbol. The json file will produce the jobs indicated below.

```json
{
  // See https://go.microsoft.com/fwlink/?LinkId=733558
  // for the documentation about the tasks.json format
  "version": "2.0.0",
  "tasks": [
    {
      "type": "gulp",
      "task": "default",
      "problemMatcher": []
    }
  ]
}
```

Typically, you would either adjust the presentation options or add an issue matcher ($eslint-stylish in this situation).

# WORKOUT PROCESSING USING PROBLEM MATCHERS

A problem matcher in Visual Studio Code can be used to process a job's output. Problem matchers scan the task output text for well-known warning or error strings and report these both in-line in the editor and on the Issues panel. The following problem matchers are included "out-of-the-box" with Visual Studio Code:

- **TypeScript**: $tsc presumes that output file names are relative to the currently open folder.
- **TypeScript Watch**: While in watch mode, the $tsc-watch function matches problems found by the tsc compiler.
- **JSHint**: $jshint incorrectly interprets file names as absolute paths.
- **JSHint Stylish**: Assumes that absolute paths for file names are provided using the $jshint-stylish variable.
- **ESLint Compact**: The output file names are presumed to be relative to the opened folder by $eslint-compact.
- **ESLint Stylish**: $eslint-stylish assumes that the output file names are relative to the opened folder.
- **Go**: $go looks for compiler errors in the go language. believes that file names are local to the opened folder.
- **CSharp and VB compilers**: These compilers' $mscompile function assumes that file names are provided as absolute paths.
- **Lessc compiler**: The Lessc compiler assumes that file names are provided as absolute paths when using $lessc.
- **Node Sass compiler**: The Node Sass compiler by default ($node-sass) specifies file names as absolute paths.

You can also refine your problem matcher, which will be covered in a later section.

# TASK-BINDING KEYBOARD SHORTCUTS

If you frequently perform a job, you can build a keyboard shortcut for it. For example, to link Ctrl+H with the Run tests task from the previous section, add the following to your keybindings. the file in json.

```json
{

  "key": "ctrl+h",

  "command": "workbench.action.tasks.runTask",

  "args": "Run tests"

}
```

# UNDERSTANDING VARIABLE SUBSTITUTION

When creating task settings, it can be useful to have a collection of predefined common variables, such as the active file ($file) or workspace root folder ($workspaceFolder). Visual Studio Code supports variable substitution inside of strings in the tasks.json file. A comprehensive collection of pre-set variables is available in the Variables Reference.

Remember that not all traits will allow for variable substitution. Only commands, args, and options specifically allow variable substitution. The TypeScript compiler receives the currently opened file when using the custom task configuration that is displayed below.

```json
{

  "label": "TypeScript compile",
```

```
  "type": "shell",

  "command": "tsc ${file}",

  "problemMatcher": ["$tsc"]

}
```

By adding $config: before the name, you can refer to your project's configuration options. For instance, the Python extension setting formatting.autopep8Path is returned via $config:python.formatting.autopep8Path.

Here is an example of a custom task setup that uses the autopep8 executable specified by the python.formatting.autopep8Path parameter to execute autopep8 on the currently open file:

```
{

  "label": "autopep8 current file",

  "type": "process",

  "command": "${config:python.formatting.autopep8Path}",

  "args": ["--in-place", "${file}"]

}
```

Use the $command:python.interpreterPath command to indicate the chosen Python interpreter that will be utilized by the Python extension for tasks.json or launch.json.

If simple variable replacement is insufficient, you may also solicit feedback from the task's user by including an inputs section in your tasks.json file.

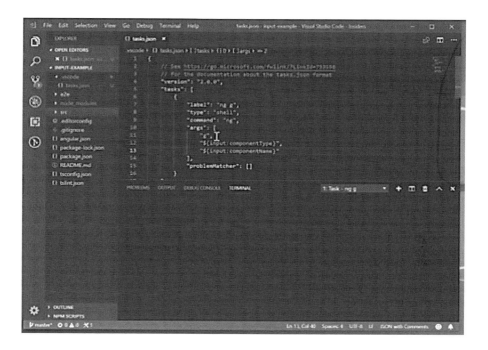

# PROPERTIES SPECIFIC TO AN OPERATING SYSTEM

The task system allows you to provide values that are specific to an operating system, like the command that needs to be executed. To accomplish this, include an operating system-specific literal in the tasks.json file and specify the required properties there.

The following command, which utilizes the Node.js executable, has distinct behavior on Windows and Linux:

*{*

*"label": "Run Node",*

173

```
"type": "process",

"windows": {

  "command": "C:\\Program Files\\nodejs\\node.exe"

},

"linux": {

  "command": "/usr/bin/node"

}}
```

For Windows, Linux, and macOS respectively, valid operating properties are windows, linux, and osx. Operating system-specific scope definitions take precedence over task- or globally-determined scope definitions when defining properties.

The definition of task attributes is also possible within the global scope. If they are present, they will only be used for the tasks for which they are defined, unless they define the same property with a different value. In the example below, a global presentation attribute specifies that each activity should be performed in a different panel:

```
{
  // See https://go.microsoft.com/fwlink/?LinkId=733558
  // for the documentation about the tasks.json format
  "version": "2.0.0",
  "presentation": {
    "panel": "new"
  },
  "tasks": [
    {
      "label": "TS - Compile current file",
      "type": "shell",
      "command": "tsc ${file}",
      "problemMatcher": ["$tsc"]
    }] }
```

# ESCAPING CHARACTER IN POWERSHELL

Unexpected space and quotation escapes may happen when PowerShell is the default shell or when a task is configured to utilize it. Unexpected escaping only occurs with cmdlets because Example 2 shows the best, cross-platform technique to achieve good escaping. Example 2 may not always be possible to follow, in which case you must carry out the manual fleeing technique shown in Example 3. The code is ignorant of any cmdlets that your command may contain. The case in which PowerShell escaping will not work is shown in the example below. Example 2 shows the top cross-platform technique for effective fleeing. Example 2 may not always be possible to follow, in which case you must carry out the manual fleeing technique shown in Example 3.

```
"tasks": [
    {
        "label": "PowerShell example 1 (unexpected escaping)",
        "type": "shell",
        "command": "Get-ChildItem \"Folder With Spaces\""
    },
    {
        "label": "PowerShell example 2 (expected escaping)",
        "type": "shell",
        "command": "Get-ChildItem",
        "args": ["Folder With Spaces"]
    },
    {
        "label": "PowerShell example 3 (manual escaping)",
        "type": "shell",
        "command": "& Get-ChildItem \\\"Folder With Spaces\\\""
    }]
```

# CHANGING A TASK'S OUTPUT ENCODING

Usually, tasks communicate with files stored on disk. If these files are saved on a disk with a different encoding than the system encoding, you must provide the encoding to use to the command run as a job. Because it depends on the operating system and shell being used, there is no solution to control this that applies to all situations. These are some suggestions and examples of how to make it work.

If you need to change the encoding, decide if it makes sense to change the default encoding for the operating system or, at the very least, change it specifically for the shell you use by changing the shell's profile file.

If you only need to change the encoding for one job, add the OS-specific command to the tasks command line. The sample that follows uses code page 437, which is the default for Windows. Code page 866 is necessary since the task displays the output of a file with Russian characters. Using cmd.exe as the default shell, the following is the task to list the file:

```json
{
    // See https://go.microsoft.com/fwlink/?LinkId=733558
    // for the documentation about the tasks.json format
    "version": "2.0.0",
    "tasks": [
        {
            "label": "more",
            "type": "shell",
            "command": "chcp 866 && more russian.txt",
            "problemMatcher": []
        } ] }
```

To complete the procedure using PowerShell, the command must be entered as chcp 866; more russian.txt. In Linux and macOS, the locale command can be used to examine the locale and change the necessary environment variables.

Below are a few examples that show the flexibility of jobs in Visual Studio Code by integrating other tools like linters and compilers.

# TYPESCRIPT TO JAVASCRIPT TRANSPILATION

An example that generates a task to translate TypeScript to JavaScript and check for any associated issues from within Visual Studio Code is provided in the TypeScript subject.

# TRANSPILING INTO CSS USING LESS AND SCSS

The CSS subject includes examples of how to create CSS files using Tasks.

- Using a file watcher to automate the build phase.
- Transpiling manually using a Build task.

# DEFINING A PROBLEM MATCHER

A few of the most popular issue matchers are included with Visual Studio Code. You might want to make your problem matcher because there are numerous compilers and linting tools available that each produce their style of errors and warnings.

The developer of the helloWorld.c program typed printf instead of prinft. The following warning will appear upon compilation with gcc:

*helloWorld.c:5:3: warning: implicit declaration of function 'prinft'*

To display a problem in the VISUAL STUDIO Code that corresponds to the message in the output, we need to create an issue matcher. Regular expressions are frequently used by problem matchers. You should be familiar with regular expressions before reading the part below.

We have discovered the ECMAScript (JavaScript)-flavored RegEx101 playground to be a fantastic tool for creating and testing regular expressions. The aforementioned warning (and errors) are captured by a matcher that looks like this:

```
{
    // The problem is owned by the cpp language service.
    "owner": "cpp",
    // The file name for reported problems is relative to the opened folder.
    "fileLocation": ["relative", "${workspaceFolder}"],
    // The actual pattern to match problems in the output.
    "pattern": {
        // The regular expression. Example to match: helloWorld.c:5:3: warning: implicit declaration of function for
        "regexp": "^(.*):(\\d+):(\\d+):\\s+(warning|error):\\s+(.*)$",
        // The first match group matches the relative file name.
        "file": 1,
        // The second match group matches the line on which the problem occurred.
        "line": 2,
        // The third match group matches the column in which the problem occurred.
        "column": 3,
        // The fourth match group matches the problem's severity. Can be ignored. Then all problems are captured as
        "severity": 4,
        // The fifth match group matches the message.
        "message": 5
    }
}
```

It is important to emphasize that the file, line, and message properties are necessary. The fileLocation property specifies whether the file paths created by the task output and matched in the problem are absolute or relative. If the task produces both absolute and relative paths, use the autoDetect file location. Using autoDetect, paths are initially verified as absolute paths; if the file doesn't exist, the path is subsequently regarded as relative.

Here is a tasks.json file that has been finished with the code from above (comments removed) wrapped around the precise task details:

```json
{
  "version": "2.0.0",
  "tasks": [
    {
      "label": "build",
      "command": "gcc",
      "args": ["-Wall", "helloWorld.c", "-o", "helloWorld"],
      "problemMatcher": {
        "owner": "cpp",
        "fileLocation": ["relative", "${workspaceFolder}"],
        "pattern": {
          "regexp": "^(.*):(\\d+):(\\d+):\\s+(warning|error):\\s+(.*)$",
          "file": 1,
          "line": 2,
          "column": 3,
          "severity": 4,
          "message": 5
        }} }] }
```

When you run it in VISUAL STUDIO Code and press Ctrl+Shift+M to receive the list of bugs, you get the output shown below:

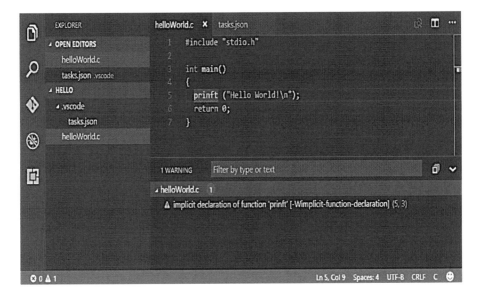

It should be noted that the GCC problem matchers are already included in the C/C++ extension, so we don't need to declare them.

A pattern may also make use of a few more qualities. Which are:

- **location**: Our general location match group can be utilized if the issue location is line, line, column, or startLine, startColumn, endLine, endColumn.
- **matchGroupIndex**: The match group index for the end line of the problem. If the compiler doesn't offer an end-line value, it may be omitted.
- **endColumn**: The index of the match group for the end column of the issue. If the compiler doesn't supply a value for the end column, it may be omitted.
- **Code**: The problem's code match the group index. If the compiler doesn't offer a code value, it may be omitted.

A problem matcher that just catches a file can also be specified. Create a pattern and specify the optional kind property to file to accomplish this. There is no need to offer a line or location property in this situation.

Remember that a functional pattern must at the very least have a matched group for files and messages if the kind attribute is set to file. If a kind property is missing or its value is set to location, a function pattern must also include a line or location property.

Moreover, keep in mind that the problem matcher does nothing more complicated than parse the command's output. If you want to interpret output written to a separate file, such as a log file, make the command you run print outlines from the separate file before it finishes processing.

# A MULTILINE PROBLEM MATCHER'S DEFINITION

Some tools can spread errors found in a source file across numerous lines, especially if fancy reporters are being used. ESLint is one instance; in its fashionable mode, it produces output that looks like this:

```
test.js
error  Missing "use strict" statement  strict
problems (1 errors, 0 warnings)
```

We must use a different regular expression to capture the file name (test.js) than the actual problem location and message (1:0 error) because our problem matcher is line-based. The "Use strict" phrase missing).

To do this, use an array of problem patterns as the pattern attribute. This defines the pattern for each line you want to match.

The output of ESLint in stylish mode corresponds to the pattern of problems listed below, although there is a small error that needs to be rectified. The file name is recorded by a first regular expression in the following code, and the line, column, severity, message, and error code are each recorded by a second regular expression:

```
{
  "owner": "javascript",
  "fileLocation": ["relative", "${workspaceFolder}"],
  "pattern": [
    {
      "regexp": "^([^\\s].*)$",
      "file": 1
    },
    {
      "regexp": "^\\s+(\\d+):(\\d+)\\s+(error|warning|info)\\s+(.*)\\s\\s+(.*)$",
      "line": 1,
      "column": 2,
      "severity": 3,
      "message": 4,
      "code": 5
    }]}
```

This pattern won't work if a resource has several issues. Take, for instance, the ESLint result displayed below.

"test.js" and "1:0 error," the second and third regular expressions in the pattern, will match. No problem is found even though the next line,

"1:9 error...", which is processed, does not match the initial regular expression.

This can be achieved by including the loop attribute in the multiline pattern's last regular expression. If the value is set to true, it instructs the task system to apply the final pattern of a multiline matcher to the lines in the output as long as the regular expression matches.

Combining the information acquired by the first pattern, which in this case matches test.js, with each of the subsequent lines, which also match the loop pattern, will result in some difficulties. This example would raise six problems.

This problem matcher reflects the fashionable problems from ESLint faithfully:

```
{
  "owner": "javascript",
  "fileLocation": ["relative", "${workspaceFolder}"],
  "pattern": [
    {
      "regexp": "^([^\\s].*)$",
      "file": 1
    },
    {"regexp": "^\\s+(\\d+):(\\d+)\\s+(error|warning|info)\\s+(.*)\\s\\s+(.*)$",
      "line": 1,
      "column": 2,
      "severity": 3,
      "message": 4,
      "code": 5,
      "loop": true
    } ] }
```

Keep in mind that if multiple issues occur on a single resource with the same line and column, only one problem will be displayed. This affects all problem matchers, not just multiline issue matchers.

# CHANGING A PREVIOUS PROBLEM MATCHER

An existing problem matcher in your tasks can be edited. json task if it almost meets your requirements. For instance, the $tsc-watch problem matcher only functions with closed documents. You can alter it to apply to all papers by taking the following actions:

```
{
    "type": "npm",
    "script": "watch",
    "problemMatcher": {
        "base": "$tsc-watch",
        "applyTo": "allDocuments"
    },
    "isBackground": true
}
```

history, file Other problem matcher attributes include location, owner, pattern, severity, and source.

## KNOWING THE HISTORY AND WATCHING THE TASK

Some applications let you keep an eye on the file system while they're running in the background and can then trigger an action when a file changes on the disk. Gulp's npm package gulp-watch offers this function. The TypeScript compiler, tsc, has a built-in command line option called watch that supports this.

To offer feedback that a background job is running in the VISUAL STUDIO Code and producing problem results, a problem matcher must use extra information to recognize these state changes in the output. Think about the tsc compiler as an example. The following extra details are printed to the console when the compiler is launched in watch mode:

```
> tsc --watch
12:30:36 PM - Compilation complete. Watching for file changes.
When a file changes on disk that contains a problem, the following output appears:
12:32:35 PM - File change detected. Starting incremental compilation...
src/messages.ts(276,9): error TS2304: Cannot find name 'candidate'.
12:32:35 PM - Compilation complete. Watching for file changes.
```

Looking at the output reveals the pattern below:

- When a file change is detected, the compiler starts. Printing to the console: starting incremental compilation
- When the compilation is finished, the compiler terminates. It is printed to the console to be looking out for file modifications.
- There have been issues between those two strings, according to reports.
- The compiler runs after the initial start without printing File change detected. Beginning incremental compilation, writing to the console.

To save this information, a problem matcher can include a backdrop property. The following describes an appropriate backdrop property for the tsc compiler:

*"background": {*

*"activeOnStart": true,*

*"beginsPattern": "^\|\|s*\|\|d{1,2}:\|\|d{1,2}:\|\|d{1,2}(?: AM\| PM)? - File change detected\|\|. Starting incremental compilation\|\|.\|\|.\|\|.",*

*"endsPattern": "^\|\|s*\|\|d{1,2}:\|\|d{1,2}:\|\|d{1,2}(?: AM\| PM)? - Compilation complete\|\|. Watching for file changes\|\|."*

*}*

The job itself must be marked as isBackground in addition to the background attribute on the problem matcher for it to continue running in the background.

# CHAPTER SEVEN

# UNDERSTANDING EMMET AND SNIPPEST

# EMMET IN VISUAL STUDIO CODE

There is no need for an extension because Microsoft Studio Code already includes support for Emmet snippets and expansion. The bulk of Emmet Actions, including expanding Emmet snippets and abbreviations, are supported by Emmet 2.0.

# HOW TO EXPAND EMMET ABBREVIATIONS AND SNIPPETS

In html, haml, pug, slim, jsx, xml, xsl, css, scss, sass, less, and stylus files as well as any language that derives from any of the aforementioned, such as handlebars and php, Emmet abbreviation, and snippet expansions are enabled by default.

An Emmet acronym will appear in the list of suggested acronyms as you begin typing it. A preview of the expansion will appear as you type if the suggestion documentation fly-out is open. The enlarged abbreviation appears in the list of suggestions arranged among the other CSS suggestions if you are in a stylesheet file.

# USING TAB FOR EMMET EXPANSIONS

Add the following setting if you want to utilize the Tab key to extend the Emmet abbreviations:

*"emmet.triggerExpansionOnTab": true*

When text contains a symbol other than an Emmet abbreviation, this setting permits indentation with the Tab key.

## Emmet when quickSuggestions are Disabled

You won't see suggestions as you type if the editor.quickSuggestions setting is disabled. By using Ctrl+Space, you can still manually activate suggestions and view the preview.

Use the following setting if you don't want to see any Emmet acronyms in suggestions:

*"emmet.showExpandedAbbreviation": "never"*

You may still enlarge your abbreviations by using the command Emmet: Expand Abbreviation. Any keyboard shortcut can be connected to the command id editor. Also, *emmet.action.expandAbbreviation*.

# UNDERSTANDING EMMET SUGGESTION ORDERING

Add the following settings to make sure Emmet's ideas are always at the top of the suggestion list:

*"emmet.showSuggestionsAsSnippets": true,*

*"editor.snippetSuggestions": "top"*

# IMPLORING EMMET ABBREVIATIONS IN OTHER FILE TYPES

Use the *emmet.includeLanguages* parameter to make the Emmet abbreviation expansion available for file formats for which it is not by default. Verify that language identifiers are used on both sides of the mapping, with the right side being the language identification of an Emmet-supported language, see the list above. For instance:

*"emmet.includeLanguages": {*

*"javascript": "javascriptreact",*

*"razor": "html",*

*"plaintext": "pug"*

*}*

Emmet may provide ideas in contexts other than HTML/CSS even though he is unfamiliar with these new languages. You can use the following setting to prevent this.

*"emmet.showExpandedAbbreviation":*
*"inMarkupAndStylesheetFilesOnly"*

It should be noted that starting with VISUAL STUDIO Code 1.15, you should use the setting emmet.includeLanguages instead if you previously used emmet.syntaxProfiles to map new file types. Emmet.syntaxProfiles is just intended for modifying the output.

## UNDERSTANDING EMMET WITH MULTI-CURSORS

The majority of Emmet actions work with multiple cursors as well:

# UNDERSTANDING FILTERS

Before being output to the editor, the expanded abbreviation is modified by filters, which are unique post-processors. Filters can be applied worldwide using the emmet.syntaxProfiles parameter or just within the current abbreviation.

Here is an illustration of the first method for applying the bem filter to all abbreviations in HTML files using the emmet.syntaxProfiles setting:

*"emmet.syntaxProfiles":*

*{*

   *"html": {*

      *"filters": "bem"*

   *}*

*}*

Add the filter to your abbreviation to produce a filter that only applies to the current abbreviation. The comment filter, for instance, will be applied to the div#page abbreviation when used as div#page|c.

# UNDERSTANDING BEM FILTER (BEM)

Bem filters come in very handy if you write HTML using the Block Element Modifier (BEM) method. Read the BEM filter in Emmet for more information on bem filters' usage. The *bem.elementSeparator* and *bem.modifierSeparator* options listed in Emmet Preferences can be used to alter this filter.

191

# UNDERSTANDING COMMENT FILTER

A comment is added around significant tags by this filter. Those tags with an id or class property are automatically considered to be "important tags."

For instance div>div#page>p.title+p|c will be expanded to:

*<div>*

   *<div id="page">*

      *<p class="title"></p>*

      *<!-- /.title -->*

      *<p></p>*

   *</div>*

   *<!-- /#page -->*

*</div>*

By utilizing the filter, you may modify this filter. comment Filter, trigger, and comment after and comment filter preferences as listed in Emmet Preferences before the filter's formatting comment.

The after preference in Code Emmet 2.0 by VISUAL STUDIO is different.

For instance, in place of:

*"emmet.preferences": {*

*"filter.commentAfter": "\n<!-- /<%= attr('id', '#') %><%= attr('class',*
*'.') %> -->"*

*}*

With VISUAL STUDIO Code, you would employ a more straightforward:

*"emmet.preferences": {*

  *"filter.commentAfter": "\n<!-- /[#ID][.CLASS] -->"*

*}*

# UNDERSTANDING THE TRIM FILTER

Only when providing abbreviations for the Emmet: Wrap with Abbreviation command is this filter effective. Wrapped lines have their line marks removed.

# USING CUSTOM EMMET SNIPPETS

A json file called snippets.json must include the definition of any custom Emmet snippets. The path to the directory holding this file should be specified in the emmet.extensionsPath parameter.

This is an illustration of what this snippets.json file's contents look like.

*{*

  *"html": {*

    *"snippets": {*

*"ull": "ul>li[id=${1} class=${2}]*2{ Will work with html, pug, haml and slim }",*

*"oll": "<ol><li id=${1} class=${2}> Will only work in html </ol>",*

*"ran": "{ Wrap plain text in curly braces }"*

*}},*

*"css": {*

*"snippets": {*

*"cb": "color: black",*

*"bsd": "border: 1px solid ${1:red}",*

*"ls": "list-style: ${1}"*

*}}}*

Using the snippets.json file to author Custom Snippets in Emmet 2.0 differs from the previous method in several ways:

Snippets Visual Studio acronyms enable both in two distinct properties called snippets and abbreviations. Snippets is the name given to the property that combines the two. Check out the default CSS and HTML snippets names of CSS snippets which may include:

When defining snippet names, avoid using (:, .) when Emmet tries to fuzzy match the given abbreviation to one of the snippets, it is utilized to divide property name and value.

snippet values for CSS Do not add; to the end of the snippet value. Based on the file type (css/less/scss, VisualStudio sass/stylus) or the emmet preference specified for *css.propertyEnd*, *sass.propertyEnd*, and *stylus.propertyEnd*, Emmet will add the trailing. Cursor location ${cursor} or ` ` can be used.

# UNDERSTANDING HTML EMMET SNIPPETS

All additional markup types, including haml and pug, are compatible with HTML custom snippets. The correct transformations can be used to produce the desired output depending on the language type when the snippet value is an acronym rather than genuine HTML.

If your snippet value is ul>li, for an unordered list with a list item, you can use the same snippet in html, haml, pug, or slim, but if it is <ul><li></li></ul>, it will only function in html files.

To get a snippet for plain text, enclose the text in quotation marks ().

# UNDERSTANDING CSS EMMET SNIPPETS

Standards for CSS The property name and value pair should be present in full in emmet snippets. All other stylesheet flavors, such as scss, less, or sass, are compatible with CSS custom snippets. Thus, avoid ending the snippet value with a trailing. Emmet will incorporate it when required, depending on whether the language calls for it.

When Emmet tries to fuzzy match the abbreviation to one of the snippets is used to distinguish property name and value. Avoid using the snippet name.

# UNDERSTANDING TAB STOPS AND CURSORS IN CUSTOM SNIPPETS

The syntax for tab stops in personalized Emmet snippets is the same as that for Textmate snippets.

- Use $1, $2, and $1:placeholder for tab stops and tab stops with placeholders, respectively.
- In the past, the cursor position in a customized Emmet snippet was indicated by the characters | or $cursor. This isn't supported anymore. Use $1 in its place.

# UNDERSTANDING EMMET CONFIGURATION

The Emmet options listed below allow you to alter how Emmet behaves in the VISUAL STUDIO Code.

- emmet.includeLanguages

To allow Emmet in the first language using the second's syntax, use this setting to add mapping between the language of your choosing and one of the supported languages for Emmet. Be sure to utilize language IDs for the mapping on both sides.

*For example:*

*"emmet.includeLanguages": {*

*"javascript": "javascriptreact",*

*"plaintext": "pug"*

*}*

- emmet.excludeLanguages

Add the language to this parameter, which accepts an array of language ID strings, if you don't want Emmet expansions to appear in that language.

- emmet.syntaxProfiles

To understand how to tailor the output of your HTML abbreviations, see Emmet Modification of the output profile. For instance:

*"emmet.syntaxProfiles": {*

   *"html": {*

     *"attr_quotes": "single"*

   *},*

   *"jsx": {*

     *"self_closing_tag": true*

   *}}*

- emmet.variables

Modify the variables Emmet snippets utilize. For instance:

*"emmet.variables": {*

   *"lang": "de",*

   *"charset": "UTF-16"*

*}*

- emmet.showExpandedAbbreviation

controls the Emmet completion and suggestion lists that appear.

# HOW TO SET VALUE DESCRIPTION

Never ever display Emmet acronyms in a language suggestion list.

Display Emmet suggestions exclusively for languages that are entirely markup and stylesheet based (such as "html," "pug," "slim," "haml," "xml," "scss," "sass," "less," and "stylus").

Always display emmet suggestions in all emmet-supported modes and for all languages for which emmet has a mapping. The includeLanguages Option.

The new Emmet implementation is not context-aware in the always mode, it should be noted. For instance, if you are updating a JavaScript React file, Emmet suggestions will be shown for both writing JavaScript and HTML.

- emmet.showAbbreviationSuggestions

Gives examples of potential emmet abbreviations. By default, it is accurate. For instance, you get suggestions for all emmet snippets beginning with li when you type li, such as link, link:css, link:favicon, etc. This helps you learn tidbits about Emmet that you might not have known about if you didn't know the Emmet cheatsheet off by heart. Not relevant when emmet or in stylesheets. The value of showExpandedAbbreviation is never.

- emmet.extensionsPath

Indicate where the directory containing the snippets is located. json file that contains your snippets.

- emmet.triggerExpansionOnTab

To enable expanding Emmet abbreviations using the Tab key, set this to true. When there is no abbreviation to expand, we use this parameter to offer the proper fallback to provide indentation.

- emmet.showSuggestionsAsSnippets

If editor.snippetSuggestions is set to true, Emmet's recommendations will be grouped with other snippets so you can sort them in any order. To guarantee that Emmet's ideas always appear above other suggestions, set this to true and editor.snippetSuggestions to top.

- emmet.preferences

With the help of this parameter, you can modify Emmet as described in Emmet Preferences. At this time, the following modifications are supported:

- css.propertyEnd
- css.valueSeparator
- sass.propertyEnd
- sass.valueSeparator
- stylus.propertyEnd
- stylus.valueSeparator
- css.unitAliases
- css.intUnit
- css.floatUnit
- bem.elementSeparator
- bem.modifierSeparator
- filter.commentBefore

- filter.commentTrigger
- filter.commentAfter
- format.noIndentTags
- format.forceIndentationForTags
- profile.allowCompactBoolean
- css.fuzzySearchMinScore

The filter's formatting. comment Emmet 2.0's after preference is different and less complicated. For instance, as opposed to the previous format

*"emmet.preferences": {*

*"filter.commentAfter": "\n<!-- /<%= attr('id', '#') %><%= attr('class', '.') %> -->"*

*}*

*You may use:*

*"emmet.preferences": {*

*"filter.commentAfter": "\n<!-- /[#ID][.CLASS] -->"*

*}*

Please submit a feature request if you desire support for any of the additional preferences listed in Emmet Preferences.

# VISUAL STUDIO CODE SNIPPETS: AN INTRODUCTION

Coders can incorporate recurring code elements like loops and conditional statements more rapidly by using code snippets as templates.

Snippets appear in a separate snippet selection and alongside other suggestions in Visual Studio Code's IntelliSense (Ctrl+Space) (Insert Snippet in the Command Palette). Tab-completion is additionally supported: To make it active, use "editor.tabCompletion": After entering "on" and a snippet prefix, press Tab to insert a snippet (trigger text).

The snippet syntax is the same as that of TextMate, except for "interpolated shell code" and the use of u, both of which are not supported.

# UNDERSTANDING THE VISUAL STUDIO BUILT-IN SNIPPETS

Just a handful of the languages that have built-in snippets in VISUAL STUDIO Code are JavaScript, TypeScript, Markdown, and PHP.

You can view a list of the snippets that are offered for the language of the current file by using the Insert Snippet command in the Command Palette. However, keep in mind that this list also includes any user snippets you have selected and any snippets provided by extensions you have installed.

# INSTALLING SNIPPETS FROM THE MARKETPLACE

The VISUAL STUDIO Code Marketplace's plugins frequently have snippets as a feature. You can search for extensions that contain snippets in the Extensions view (Ctrl+Shift+X) by using the @category: "snippets" filter.

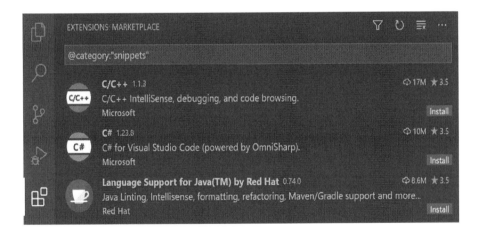

To access the new snippets, restart Visual Studio Code after installing any extensions you intend to use.

# UNDERSTANDING HOW TO ESTABLISH YOUR SNIPPETS

You can define your snippets with or without an extension. To add or change your snippets, go to File > Preferences (Mac OS X: Code > Preferences) and choose Configure User Snippets. Next, select the language (by language identifier) in which you want the snippets to appear. Alternatively, if you want them to appear in all languages, select the Create Global Snippets file option. You receive creation and maintenance of the underlying snippets files from VISUAL STUDIO Code.

Snippets files are written in JSON, support C-style comments, and can define an endless number of snippets. Multiline editing is made easier via snippets, which also support the majority of TextMate syntax for dynamic behavior. Also, depending on the context of their insertion, they intelligently format whitespace. The following gives an example of a JavaScript for loop snippet:

```
// in file 'Code/User/snippets/javascript.json'
{
  "For Loop": {
    "prefix": ["for", "for-const"],
    "body": ["for (const ${2:element} of ${1:array}) {", "\t$0", "}"],
    "description": "A for loop."
  }
}
```

In the earlier illustration:

- The snippet is titled "For Loop." If no description is provided, IntelliSense is used to display it.
- The snippet is displayed by IntelliSense when one or more trigger words are defined in the prefix. Prefixes are used to match substrings, so in this case, "fc" might match "for-const."
- Body is one or more lines of text that will be joined to form several lines when placed. The context in which the sample is used will determine how newlines and embedded tabs are formatted.
- The optional description provides a synopsis of the sample that IntelliSense has shown.

Also, there are three placeholders in the body of the aforementioned example (stated in traversal order): $:array, $:2:element, and $0. Using Tab, you may swiftly advance to the following placeholder, where you can alter it or move on to the one after it. The string that follows the colon is the default text, for example, element in $2:element (if any). The order of the placeholders is increasing starting with one and ending with zero, an optional special case that always comes last and leaves snippet mode with the cursor in the specified location.

# UNDERSTANDING FILE TEMPLATE SNIPPETS

If your snippet is intended to populate or replace a file's contents, you can add the isFileTemplate attribute to its declaration. When you use the Snippets: Populate File from Snippet command in a new or existing file, file template snippets are shown in a menu.

# UNDERSTANDING SNIPPET SCOPE

Only pertinent snippets are suggested since snippets are scoped. There are two ways to scope snippets:

- The language or languages that excerpts are limited to (possibly all).
- The project(s) that the scoped snippets apply to (probably all).

# UNDERSTANDING LANGUAGE SNIPPET SCOPE

Each snippet is scoped to one, several, or all ("global") languages depending on the language in which it is defined.

- A file of linguistic snippets.
- An international snippet file.

Single-language user-defined snippets are defined in the language's snippet file (for example, javascript.json), which you can access through Preferences by language identifier: Set up the user snippets. A snippet cannot be viewed unless the language for which it is specified is changed.

All "global" snippet files, which are also accessible through Preferences and are JSON with the file suffix.code-snippets: Create multilingual and worldwide user-defined snippets by setting up user snippets. An additional scope property that accepts one or more language identifiers and restricts the languages for which the snippet is available may be present in a snippet definition in a global snippet file. If the scope property is not given, the global snippet is present in all languages.

A language-specific snippet file is used to specify the vast majority of user-created snippets because they are language-specific.

# UNDERSTANDING PROJECT SNIPPET SCOPE

You can also scope a global snippets JSON file with the file extension .code-snippets to your project. The preference's Create Snippets file for "..." option: Visual Studio Code's Configure User Snippets dropdown option generates snippets for project folders, which are then saved in the project's root folder. By using project snippet files, snippets can be shared with all people taking part in a project. Project-folder snippets can be scoped to specific languages using the scope attribute, just like global snippets can.

# UNDERSTANDING SNIPPET SYNTAX

The body of a snippet can employ certain structures to manage cursors and the text that is being added. Supported features and their respective syntaxes include:

- **Tabstops**: You can shift the editor cursor inside a snippet by using tabstops. To indicate the cursor locations, use $1 and $2. In contrast to $0, which represents the final cursor point, the number indicates the order in which tabstops will be visited. The same tabstop appears more than once and is linked to and updated simultaneously.
- **Placeholders**: Tabstops containing values, such as $"1:foo," are called placeholders. The placeholder text will be added and chosen to make it simple to edit. You can layer placeholders, for example, $:another $:placeholder.
- **Choice**: Options are possible values for placeholders. The syntax is an enumeration of values separated by commas and encased in a pipe, as in $1|one,two,three|. The user will be presented with choices after inserting the snippet and selecting the placeholder, prompting them to select one of the values.
- **Variables**: A variable's value can be inserted using $name or $name:default. The empty string or the variable's default value is added if it is not set. When a variable is undefined, or when

its name isn't defined, its name is inserted and it becomes a placeholder.

You can utilize the following variables:

- **TM_SELECTED_TEXT**: Either the empty string or the text that is currently selected.
- **TM_CURRENT_LINE**: Information about the current line's content.
- **TM_CURRENT_WORD**: The text within the cursor's current word or an empty string.
- **TM_LINE_INDEX**: The line number is based on a zero index.
- **TM_LINE_NUMBER**: The line number is based on a single index.
- **TM_FILENAME**: The current document's filename.
- **TM_FILENAME BASE**: The current document's filename without any extensions.
- **TM_DIRECTORY**: The current document's directory
- **TM FILEPATH**: The current document's whole file path.
- **RELATIVE_FILEPATH**: The current document's file path as it relates to the workspace or folder that is now open.
- **CLIPBOARD**: The items on your clipboard are listed under.
- **WORKSPACE_NAME**: The name of the workspace or folder that was just opened.
- **WORKSPACE_FOLDER**: The location of the workspace or folder that was opened.
- **CURSOR_INDEX**: The cursor number is based on a zero index.
- **CURSOR_NUMBER**: The cursor number is based on a single index.

For inserting the current date and time:

- **CURRENT_YEAR**: The year that is currently in effect.

- **CURRENT_YEAR_SHORT**: The last two digits of the current year.
- **CURRENT_MONTH**: The month as a two-digit number (for instance, "02").
- **CURRENT MONTH NAME**: The month's complete name (for instance, "July").
- **CURRENT_MONTH_NAME_SHORT**: The month's short name (for instance, "Jul").
- **CURRENT_DATE**: The current date is two digits (for instance, "08").
- **CURRENT_DAY_NAME**: The day's name (for instance, "Monday").
- **CURRENT_DAY_NAME_SHORT**: The day's abbreviated name (for instance, "Mon").
- **CURRENT_HOUR**: The hour is represented by a 24-hour clock.
- **CURRENT_MINUTE**: The second digit of the current minute.
- **CURRENT_SECOND**: The second has two digits at the moment.
- **CURRENT_SECONDS_UNIX**: The duration since the Unix epoch in seconds.

To insert random values:

```
RANDOM 6 random Base-10 digits
RANDOM_HEX 6 random Base-16 digits
UUID A Version 4 UUID
```

Respecting the language being used while including line or block comments

> **BLOCK_COMMENT_START**: Example output: in PHP /* or in HTML <!--
> **BLOCK_COMMENT_END**: Example output: in PHP */ or in HTML -->
> **LINE_COMMENT**: Example output: in PHP //

The code snippet below inserts "Hello World" in HTML pages and "/* Hello World */" in JavaScript files:

```
{
  "hello": {
    "scope": "javascript,html",
    "prefix": "hello",
    "body": "$BLOCK_COMMENT_START Hello World $BLOCK_COMMENT_END"
  }
}
```

# VARIABLE TRANSFORMATION

Transformations allow you to alter a variable's value before entering it. The definition of a transformation is composed of three components:

- A regular expression that matches either the empty string (if the variable can't be resolved) or the value of the variable.
- A "format string" that permits the usage of reference groups for regular expression matching.
- Parameters passed to the regular expression; the format string supports basic changes as well as conditional insertion.

When the name of the current file is added without its conclusion in the example below, foo.txt becomes foo.

*${TM_FILENAME/(.*)||.+$/$1/}*

# UNDERSTANDING PLACEHOLDER-TRANSFORM

While moving to the next tab stop, a transformation of a placeholder, such as a variable-transform, permits editing the text that is substituted for the placeholder. The newly added text is compared to the regular expression, and the match or matches are transformed to the replacement format text depending on the options. Each occurrence of a placeholder can independently indicate its transformation using the value of the initial placeholder. The structure of placeholder transforms is the same as that of variable transforms.

# UNDERSTANDING GRAMMAR

Below is a link to the EBNF (extended Backus-Naur form) for snippets. With the backslash, you can escape the $, and (). The comma and pipe characters can also escape within appropriate components thanks to the backslash.

```
any ::= tabstop | placeholder | choice | variable | text
tabstop ::= '$' int
          | '${' int '}'
          | '${' int transform '}'
placeholder ::= '${' int ':' any '}'
choice      ::= '${' int '|' text (',' text)* '|}'
variable    ::= '$' var | '${' var '}'
          | '${' var ':' any '}'
          | '${' var transform '}'
transform   ::= '/' regex '/' (format | text)+ '/' options
format      ::= '$' int | '${' int '}'
          | '${' int ':' '/upcase' | '/downcase' | '/capitalize' | '/camelcase' | '/pascalcase' '}'
          | '${' int ':+' if '}'
          | '${' int ':?' if ':' else '}'
          | '${' int ':-' else '}' | '${' int ':' else '}'
regex   ::= JavaScript Regular Expression value (ctor-string)
options ::= JavaScript Regular Expression option (ctor-options)
var   ::= [_a-zA-Z] [_a-zA-Z0-9]*
int   ::= [0-9]+
tex   ::= .*
if   ::= text
else   ::= text
```

# UNDERSTANDING TEXTMATE SNIPPETS

You may also use pre-existing TextMate snippets with VISUAL STUDIO Code (.tmSnippets). See the Using TextMate Snippets topic in our Extension API section for further details.

# KEYBINDINGS AND HOW TO ASSIGN THEM TO SNIPPETS

Custom keybindings can be made to insert particular snippets. Keybindings are open. Add a keybinding giving "snippet" as an additional argument to the json file that describes all of your keybindings (Open the keyboard shortcuts file as a preference):

```
{

  "key": "cmd+k 1",

  "command": "editor.action.insertSnippet",

  "when": "editorTextFocus",

  "args": {

    "snippet": "console.log($1)$0"

}}
```

The keybinding will activate the Insert Snippet command, but instead of prompting you to select a snippet, it will insert the one that is already there. You describe the custom keybinding, as usual, using a keyboard shortcut, command ID, and an optional when clause context for when the keyboard shortcut is activated.

Instead, you can specify your snippet inline using the langId and name arguments rather than the snippet argument value. In the example below, the myFaVisual Studionippet for csharp-files is chosen by using the langId option, which also chooses the language for which the snippet identified by name is put.

```
{
  "key": "cmd+k 1",
  "command": "editor.action.insertSnippet",
  "when": "editorTextFocus",
  "args": {
    "langId": "csharp",
    "name": "myFaVisual Studionippet"
  }}
```

# CONCLUSION

With the constant evolution of technology, Visual Studio Code will become increasingly important in the software development process. It is undoubtedly "THE THING" to stay ahead of the competition in this constantly expanding IT industry with its constantly evolving capabilities and soon-to-be-added new features, which will enable users to work with it from anywhere.

# INDEX

## A

Actions, 187
activity, 31, 65
Activity, 36, 73
**Activity Bar**, 36, 73
**Adding tools**, 26
Advanced, 83
API, 3, 80
app, 14
applications, 3, 29, 33
apps, 32, 33, 77
ASP, 30
ASP.NET, 30
asynchronous, 30
Azure, 32, 35

## B

background, 59, 185, 186
Bar, 48
beginners, 29
Blazor, 30
bootstrapper, 6
brackets, 29
breakpoint, 142
built-in, 145

## C

C#,, 3
C++,, 3
Case, 90, 91
**Changing fonts**, 20
cheatsheet, 198
checkbox, 62
CLIPBOARD, 207
cloud, 32, 93
cmd, 211
code, 3, 9, 14, 28, 31, 34, 35,
    77, 79, 80, 93, 123, 181, 209
Code, 5, 14, 16, 29, 36, 56, 57,
    59, 60, 64, 74, 80, 81, 82, 84,
    93, 103, 119, 123, 141, 145,
    155, 177, 178, 181, 187, 190,
    192, 193, 196, 213
Color, 57, 58, 59
**color scheme**, 16
color theme designer, 16
colored, 43
command, 14, 16, 93, 156,
    159, 164, 165, 168, 171, 172,
    174, 188, 193, 204, 211
command-line, 93
commands, 47, 74, 89
comment, 191, 192, 200

compile, 171

compiler, 170, 181, 185

completion, 31, 198

component, 80

conditions, 84

configuration, 90, 103, 146, 172

configurations, 48, 80

configured, 15

console, 3, 74, 139, 184, 185, 211

CONSOLE, 74, 144

Continue, 35

Create, 33, 78, 79, 181

Cursor, 195

customizations, 63

**Customizing fonts**, 19

**Customizing panels**, 25

**Customizing the tool bar**, 23

---

### D

databases, 33

debug, 74

Debug, 34, 74

debugger, 80, 123, 142, 145

debuggers, 145

debugging, 36, 74, 123, 127

decorations, 80

**default themes**, 17

dependent, 71

detection, 29, 156

developer, 178

developers, 29, 32

development, 3, 72, 80, 213

Development, 3

DevOps, 35

directory, 71, 78, 193, 199, 207

documentation, 80, 188

download, 5, 6, 15

downloaded, 15

downloads, 5

Drag, 29, 37, 50, 113

---

### E

echo, 165

Editing, 62

editor, 36, 37, 39, 47, 48, 51, 52, 59, 80, 83, 89, 90, 93, 139, 188, 189, 191, 199, 206, 211

Editor, 36, 60, 65, 87, 88

EDITORS, 43

element, 43, 204

Emmet, 187, 188, 189, 190, 191, 192, 193, 194, 195, 196, 197, 198, 199, 200

environment, 3, 35, 56, 72, 139

Environment, 3

errors, 43, 165, 178

excerpts, 205

executable, 172

execution, 142

Expand, 188

expansion, 187, 188, 189

215

Explorer, 36, 37, 43, 85, 108

expressions, 178

extensions, 29, 64, 80, 119, 123, 142, 207

Extensions, 64

## F

features, 29, 30, 32, 72, 81, 119, 123, 213

file, 6, 15, 30, 37, 43, 47, 48, 78, 79, 80, 81, 82, 83, 113, 139, 155, 159, 169, 170, 172, 173, 181, 185, 188, 189, 190, 193, 194, 198, 199, 204, 205, 207, 211

File, 57, 60, 79, 81, 185, 204, 211

FILENAME, 207, 209

FILEPATH, 207

files, 15, 35, 36, 38, 47, 77, 78, 79, 80, 81, 82, 84, 85, 187, 191, 195, 209

filter, 191, 192, 193, 199, 200

filters, 191

fingertips, 30

Flatpak, 15, 16

focus, 63, 89, 165

folder, 6, 35, 36, 43, 48, 78, 79, 80, 81, 82, 83, 84, 85, 139, 170, 207

folders, 78, 80, 84

functionalities, 30

fuzzy, 194, 195

## G

Git, 30, 93, 113, 119

GitHub, 29, 35, 93, 103

global, 60, 153

groups, 63

GUI, 3

## H

handlebars, 187

## I

icons, 43, 77

ID, 193, 197, 200

IDE, 3, 36, 72

indentation, 39, 188, 199

Install, 8

installation, 6, 7, 8, 15, 32

installed, 6

installer, 6

instructions, 5, 15

integrated, 3, 71, 72, 119

Integrated, 3, 119, 164

IntelliCode, 31

IntelliSense, 59, 123, 159

INTERFACE, 35

Issues, 93, 103, 165

## J

JavaScript, 3, 177, 178, 198, 209
JSON, 137
Jupyter, 29, 123

## K

keyboard, 29, 57, 188

## L

languages, 3, 189, 196, 198, 205
launch, 9, 36, 60, 74, 127, 141, 146, 172
layout, 29
License, 7
LINE, 207
link, 29, 198
Linux, 14, 15, 29, 60, 174
Live, 36
location, 78, 82, 181, 195, 207

## M

Mac, 9, 29, 37
machine, 5, 113
macOS, 3, 57, 174
Maintain, 80
manage, 98
**Managing window layouts**, 27
mapping, 189, 196, 198

Marketplace, 29
matcher, 178, 181, 186
matches, 84
matching, 39
Menu, 48
Mercurial, 119
MERGE, 73, 115
Microsoft, 3, 7, 187
modification, 43
MSBuild, 77

## N

navigate, 36
navigation, 63, 78
NET, 30
**Node**, 127, 173
npm, 157

## O

Online, 3
operating, 5, 174
options, 60, 65, 74, 88, 156, 159, 172, 191, 196
Options, 48, 60, 83, 206
OS, 15, 57
outline, 43
output, 74, 145, 165, 170, 178, 190, 191, 195, 197
Output, 72

## P

package, 15
panel, 164, 165
**panels**, 26
**Panels**, 36
parameter, 142, 172, 189, 191, 193, 197, 199
pattern, 151, 180, 181
permits, 188
picker, 57, 153
platform, 33, 81, 93
preferences, 48, 59, 80, 192, 193, 199, 200
Preferences, 57, 60, 191, 192, 199, 200
Preset, 60
processors, 191
Profiles, 29
programming, 3, 35
project, 35, 36, 48, 77, 78, 80, 81, 172, 205
projects, 30, 35, 78
properties, 159, 174, 194
Pull, 93, 98
Python, 3, 123, 172

## Q

Quick, 31, 37, 52, 156

## R

Razor, 30

Remote, 108, 123
reorder, 50
REPL, 144
Replace, 85
repositories, 108
repository, 73
Requests, 93, 98
Run, 74, 153, 168, 171, 173
**runOn**, 167
runOptions, 159
runtime, 145

## S

sass, 187, 194, 195, 198, 199
Save, 80
SCM, 119
scope, 174, 204
search, 16, 29, 65, 82, 83, 84, 85, 88, 89
Search, 30, 44, 83, 85, 87, 88
selector, 57
services, 3
setting, 39, 52, 59, 141, 165, 172, 188, 189, 190, 191, 196
settings, 29, 39, 48, 51, 57, 59, 60, 62, 63, 64, 84, 85, 113, 127, 141, 189
shell, 172
shortcuts, 29, 57, 78
**Side Bar**, 36
Snap, 14

snippets, 187, 193, 194, 195, 196, 197, 198, 199, 204, 205, 211

Snippets, 194, 204

software, 3, 14, 16, 213

Software, 14

sort, 199

source, 34, 35, 93, 119

source code, 19

source code editor, 19

Source Control, 63, 73

splitting, 37

Splitting, 71

Start, 9

Status Bar, 36

suggestions, 188, 198, 199

support, 14, 15, 16, 187, 200

supports, 14, 16

switch, 50

syntax, 59, 84, 142, 196, 206

## T

template, 204

terminal, 29, 71, 164, 165

Terminal, 29, 153, 164, 165

terminals, 71

Terminate, 139

Terms, 7

Testing, 123

theme, 57, 59

Theme, 57, 58, 59

themes, 56

toggle, 43, 85

toolbars, 21

tools, 30, 31, 178

trigger, 103, 192

TypeScript, 153, 170, 171, 177

## U

Ubuntu, 14, 15

unique, 64, 80, 191

updates, 29, 30

User, 3, 60, 141

## V

VB, 3

version, 5, 15, 30

View, 72, 164

views, 29, 36, 80

visual studio, 19

Visual studio, 17

Visual Studio, 3, 5, 6, 9, 14, 16, 29, 30, 31, 32, 35, 36, 48, 56, 57, 59, 60, 64, 77, 78, 80, 81, 82, 84, 93, 119, 123, 141, 145, 155, 177, 178, 194, 213

## W

warnings, 43, 165, 178

webRoot, 151

website, 93

Websites, 3

window, 7, 28, 35, 36, 65, 72, 80, 81

**window layout**, 28

Windows, 3, 5, 6, 29, 30, 60, 77, 174

**Working with document**, 26

workspace, 39, 48, 60, 80, 81, 83, 85, 139, 207

Made in United States
Troutdale, OR
02/03/2024

17416756R00128